ALSO BY LAURIE NOTARO

The Idiot Girls' Action-Adventure Club

Autobiography of a Fat Bride

I Love Everybody

We Thought You Would Be Prettier

An Idiot Girl's
CHRISTMAS

An Idiot Girl's
CHRISTMAS

*True Tales from the Top
of the Naughty List*

LAURIE NOTARO

VILLARD

NEW YORK

Published in the United States by Villard Books,
an imprint of The Random House Publishing Group,
a division of Random House, Inc., New York.

VILLARD and "V" CIRCLED Design are registered
trademarks of Random House, Inc.

"There's a Gun Somewhere Under the Christmas Tree"
(originally published as "Hair of the Dog") and "Jingle Hell"
previously appeared in *Autobiography of a Fat Bride* by Laurie
Notaro (2003), and "Christmas Death Trap" (originally
published as "For the Birds") previously appeared in *The Idiot
Girls' Action-Adventure Club* by Laurie Notaro (2002), both
published by Villard Books, an imprint of The Random House
Publishing Group, a division of Random House, Inc., New York.

ISBN: 1-4000-6436-8

Printed in the United States of America
on acid-free paper

www.villard.com

2 4 6 8 9 7 5 3 1

First Edition

Book design by Jo Anne Metsch

To Idiot Girls everywhere

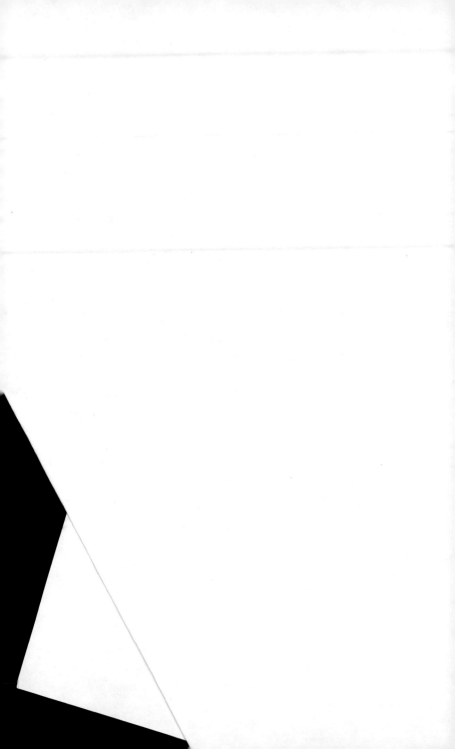

Contents

Contents

An Idiot Girl's
CHRISTMAS

What I Really Want
for Christmas

This year, I've finally come face-to-face with the truth: I'm getting crap for Christmas. I guess it really shouldn't bother me, and should come as absolutely no surprise. I always get crap for Christmas. I, however, do not get as much crap as my friend Kate does when she goes home to Minnesota for the holidays, and then she has to haul all of the crap halfway across the continental United States.

This year, to avoid the disappointment of asking for a leather jacket and getting a windbreaker with a reindeer on it instead (last year's tragedy), Kate has determined that she will beat her family at their own game. She is a genius.

We were out to dinner when she unfolded her ultimate plan of brilliancy. "Last night, my mom called and asked what I wanted for Christmas," Kate said. "And I thought for a minute, and I really wanted to say, 'It doesn't matter, because you'll just get me the first thing you see with a sale sticker on it at Wal-Mart.' And then I decided, why be disappointed? I'm never going to get what I ask for, so I told my mom, 'What I really want is some dish towels with puffy decals on them, preferably of a Christmas character, the cheapest washcloths ever made, and the biggest, whitest pairs of underwear you can find at Sears. That's what I want.' "

According to Kate, her mother giggled with delight. "Ooooh," she cooed, "that will be easy!"

So I'm taking the same route. This year, I've made my list and I've checked it twice, so this one's for you, Mom, who never fails to get me enough white cotton briefs to outfit a convent for a whole year, and other people who see fit to unload the Crap Wagon on me on what is SUPPOSED to be the Happiest Day of the Year. It is the DISNEYLAND OF DAYS, but I always end up hauling shit home that belongs only on a shelf at Goodwill. And no, it is not the thought that counts when the thought is "Only a little is missing. She'll never know I used this."

WHAT I REALLY WANT FOR CHRISTMAS
by Laurie Notaro

What I really want for Christmas is a Big Mouth Billy Bass or a Travis the Singing Trout. The more the better, especially now that they're available in outlet stores for ninety-nine cents, being that their novelty has worn a rut into the ground deeper than the Oregon Trail. I could hang them on my wall all together, like they would be in real life in a lake. They are the funniest things I've ever seen, and I never get tired of hearing them sing.

Pick out a whimsical hat for me, something you've never seen another person wear that just beckons to you from the hat stand as you point to it and exclaim in uncontained excitement, "THAT is Laurie!" If it resembles something a character from the classic ensemble Fat Albert or Captain Stubing of *The Love Boat* would wear or something you've seen on a pimp, it probably belongs on my head. If it has feathers on it, all the better— after all, who knows my style better than people who don't even know that acrylic gives me hives, and will be expecting me to wear it when they come to visit.

Always on my list is a scrumptious delicacy from my mother's favorite Wax Candle Baked Goods store. I don't know where my mother found a wax store that specializes in baked-goods and pastry candles, but she did. Good work, Mom! Mmmm, mmmmm, just imagine a whole box of cupcakes—moist, rich chocolate cake underneath a virtual mushroom cloud of marvelous buttercream frosting, bursting with a delicious, irresistible cupcake smell. And I mean bursting, filling up rooms of the house like you've just baked them. It's the perfect diet food, because biting into one is like biting into Jennifer Lopez's double-decker ass at Madame Tussaud's, kinda like sinking your choppers into a thick, dense bar of Irish Spring—without the flavor. Yummy yummy. Because having fake cupcakes that smell like real cupcakes around your house all day long every day is just what a fat girl needs to make her carrot-stick-and-cottage-cheese lunch last and last and last until it's time to peel back the film on her steaming, overcooked-to-the-point-of-dehydration Lean Cuisine dinner. Yummy. I can't say it enough. YUMMY.

Another thing I really want is chunks of hair from the hair carts at the mall. I want extensions, braids, and a big fake bun. How intriguing would I be, showing up every day with a new hairstyle? One day short, one day long, one day curly, and one day with cornrows? Please, make me beautiful (and mysterious!) (and blond!) (and redheaded!) (and raven-haired!)! Gimme a head with hair, long beautiful hair! Shining, gleaming, streaming, flaxen, waxen, but most importantly, hair I *never have to wash.*

This next request may seem impossible, but I know it's not! I would love every article of clothing you can think of with Tweety Bird on it that you haven't already given me. Yes, everything! Go to that Warner Bros. clearance rack and just plunder! T-shirts, sweatshirts, socks, a coat, a hat, a windbreaker, sweatpants, tote bag, coasters—anything with Tweety Bird on it would be just incredible, even though I'm not the one who was so fascinated with Tweety Bird that I had him tattooed on my shoulder, it's my husband's ex-girlfriend.

Of course, I would enjoy nothing more than getting some really cheap bath crystals, so I could use them when I take a shower because I don't have a bathtub. If you could get some that smell like Pine-Sol or an old lady's teeth, I would squeal with glee! Happy piglet would I be. What else would be more relaxing than tossing up a handful of crystals and running around my shower stall so they hit me and stick to me like kitty litter?

Oh, and yes, you guessed it, Christmas socks! If there's anything that says, "Let's celebrate the birthday of your Christian Lord," it's an acrylic knit with metallic thread and a reinforced toe. I love Christmas socks! I love all kinds of Christmas socks—socks with snowmen, snowflakes, Santa, trees—and if I've been really good this year, get me ones with the word "Believe!" stitched right up the side. I BELIEVE in Christmas socks! Christmas socks with bells? Jingly, jolly, and rockin' with holly! If you could score Baby Jesus socks, my God. Literally! Could I ever come down off that cloud? While you're in the foot aisle at Safeway buying my Christmas present, take a step to the left and grab a can of Tough Actin' Tinactin, too, because I'll want to wear these socks so much you'll have to kill me to get them off my feet, and eventually I'll need something for the itch and decomposition of my toes.

Don't forget a block of monogrammed Lucite, especially one with the meaning of my name documented on it to clear up the mystery and help ground my self-identity: "Laurie: Feminine form of the Late Latin name *Laurus*, which means 'laurel,' which was used to create victors' garlands. Saint Laura was a ninth-century Spanish martyr, a nun who was thrown into a vat of molten lead by the Moors." Ho ho ho! That's right. Nothing says love, class, and Happy Holidays like a clear chunk of plastic teamed up with my name and the inspiring tale of a nun who was boiled to death like a lobster.

If all of the Lucite blocks are already sold out (you can't take astonishing gifts for granted, you know), do me a favor; go the extra mile and bestow upon me a Rubik's Cube with your photo on all sides! What's better than one photo of you? Why, SIX of them! What fun it would be to writhe in the eternal task of spending my spare time putting six of your heads on six of the appropriate bodies! Grand fun, I tell you, grand. The only way I'd have more fun is if I was beating my arms against my body while cloaked in a killer bee colony intent on tickling me all the way into an anaphylactic coma!

If you're in a jam and suddenly realize that my name has vanished from your shopping list and you never ordered that Six Sides of Me, Me, Me, Me, Me, and Then Me Rubik's Cube, fear not, do not curse yourself; something from your house is fine, preferably if it's used. Who wouldn't mind a little pre-loved bath gel or lotion, or soap that you've found a little too fragrant for your tastes? In the immortal words of George W. Bush during the time of overwhelming insurgent attacks in a hostile country, BRING IT ON! Shampoo that's not for you, pour some sugar on me! I understand that you've merely pretested it to make sure it lives up to the standards you set for giving gifts. I totally understand that. Kind of like when people would taste food for kings to make sure it's not poisoned, except in this case, you spit a little back on the plate is all. That's all. Just a little spit. What's a little spit in a heartfelt Christmas gift? So little that you almost can't tell it's hardly there at all. Hardly. I would also love little sample soaps and tiny bottles of shampoo and conditioner from hotels. Makes me feel like I've been on vacation without the expense or the hassle of enjoyment.

And lastly, FREE GIFTS that you've received for buying something you wanted are always welcome in my Christmas stocking! After all, if you're getting a free gift with something you bought, why pay for mine? Why should you fork out moolah for my gift just because I forked out moolah for yours? The look on our faces is payment enough when we open the Choo-Choo Train wall clock that you got as a bonus when you bought the "Riding the Rails" Hobo Train Set you've just spent the last hour showing us in great detail despite the fact that we have already seen it multiple times on television since the commercial offering the free Choo-Choo clock with purchase is on what you could term "heavy rotation" during the holiday season. Choo choo! Choo Choo! Every quarter, half, and full hour on the hour, choo choo! Enough to make a peaceful man take up shootin', or to understand why you'd pass on a perfectly good free gift like this. Free gifts are not always pleasant, let's remember, like parking tickets and VD.

Well, I can't wait for Christmas now, as I'm sure everything on my wish list will be bought, ordered, or scavenged from the musty, danky hall closet and all of my dreams will come true. Except for the one in which I'm in a business meeting eating a doughnut and when I look down to brush off the crumbs (oh, there are *always* crumbs) there's just a sprinkling of coconut flakes over my big, bare, naked boobs, although I am wearing a watch and a Hope Eternal Diamonique pendant from QVC that my mom got me last year. I hope that dream better not come true. That pendant is so full of fake sparkle it could bring in planes.

Merry Christmas!
Laurie

P.S. Oh, I forgot one thing: I sure could use some more white cotton briefs, and the bigger the better! We used some of last year's supply to cover bushes during the last freeze, and also as sheets for the guest bedroom. Toss in some nylon panties, too, because we're thinking about taking up skydiving.

Helpful Tips on How to Throw an Unforgettable Holiday Party and Die Alone in Six Easy Steps

I was walking by the TV last week when an episode of a local lifestyle show caught my eye. The featured guests, two police officers, were explaining how several factors were essential to make your holiday party a successful one, and that's when I eagerly pulled up a chair to watch uninterrupted.

Oh, good, I thought, they're going to fork over the recipe for Johnny Law's Jungle Juice, and I got ready to write it all down, and this is what they said:

Holiday Prevention Information for those
of you who are HOSTING Parties:
· Serve high-protein food, and offer nonalcoholic beverages.

- Encourage guests to designate a driver or offer alternative transportation.
- Never serve alcohol to those under the age of twenty-one.
- Don't let guests mix their own drinks, and "close the bar" ninety minutes before the party ends.
- Report suspected drunk drivers IMMEDIATELY to area police.

Now, I don't know how many parties those cops have been to in their lives, but in my book, those aren't tips on how to have a successful party; those are a step-by-step list of "Six Easy Steps to Become a Social Pariah and Ensure a Death So Lonely That Only the Stench of Your Corpse Will Be of Consequence to Anybody."

Okay, now the "serve high-protein food" part I can totally agree with, because if you ever lose me at a party, find the cheese platter. Sure, some people call it filler, but I call it "Little Squares of Love," and as far as I'm concerned, there's no reason to answer the door if you don't have little orange cubes with frilly toothpicks stuck in them behind it.

The alternative transportation part—sure, fine, fine, whatever. You want alternative transportation, hire a limo, but all you're getting from me is the recitation of "252-5252 Yellow Cab" and my phone in your hand. I mean, I'm throwing a *party* here, I'm not running FedEx. If you positively, absolutely have to be back home overnight, dude, make some Mormon friends, but don't count on me to be your ride.

Then there's the "never serve alcohol to those under the age of twenty-one" clause, which I guess I can agree with because I'm married, but if I was still dating, I mean, that's like throwing away half of the sea full of very strapping, fetching fish. Perfectly good talent going right to waste. But hey, you know, I want to throw a successful Holiday Prevention Information party, and that means no drunk, sexy, virile younguns, apparently.

And then we have the "Don't let guests mix their own drinks, and 'close the bar' ninety minutes before the party ends" rule.

Honestly, I'm not even sure what I should say first about this.

Um, you know, the last time I had a party that ended at a specific time, I got hit after my friends went home because Rhonda Legarski attached the tape on the tail of the donkey to my mother's brand-new red-velvet-flocked wallpaper.

Ninety minutes before the party ends? How are you supposed to know when THAT is? I mean, when the host flies out a window or is seen passed out in a bathtub or is escorted away in handcuffs, THEN I guess you can say, "Wow, we were supposed to stop drinking, like, ninety minutes ago," but come ON, man! Do you see me with my own TV show talking to dead people? I'm no psychic! I didn't go to school for that! How do I know when the party is going to end? That's a lot of pressure for a partygoer, you know! Most of the time I'm not even sure if it's still P.M., let alone trying to figure out when every alcoholic at the party is going to burst into a pumpkin!

Surely my FAVORITE has to be "Report suspected drunk drivers IMMEDIATELY to area police." Oh, sure, yeah. Especially if you want to have another party next year. Talk about having five pounds of cheese cubes on your hands. Absolutely, everyone is going to go to your house for a party, especially when you got seven people arrested last year in your driveway. "Let's go to Neil's party this year, I think it will be a whole lot more fun than turning myself in," or "You know, Sharon's party is the place to be if you ever wondered what a Field Sobriety Test was like." Sure, it's a good idea, but only if you're running for office.

So beware, folks, if you're invited anywhere this season, you might want to ask if you can peek at the Party Manifesto before you commit to an evening of fun that rivals time spent in a holding pen at the county jail.

Well, at least there you could say, "You know, you should have stopped drinking ninety minutes ago."

Naughty or Nice

Naughty or nice.

Naughty or nice.

It looked like I had a decision to make.

I wavered back and forth as I approached the line at the checkout as it grew, exponentially, by the second.

If you've ever been to a do-it-yourself craft store in the weeks preceding the holiday season, I can fully confirm that you have experienced the seventh circle of hell.

All I needed was a $1.49 chunky rubber stamp in the shape of a jingle bell to make some Christmas cards, and I found myself fourth in line, right behind a lady with dyed ratty hair. Despite the two cashier's stations facing each other, some genius had decided that we were all going to form one line, which stretched out into the aisle and placed me in front of a rack of twinkle-light nets on sale for $2.99. After the third Glue Gun Queen grazed my shin with her cart and caught the bottom of my backpack purse with her elbow, I turned around and bellowed a loud "EXCUSE ME," just to prove that I hadn't taken my invisible pills that morning.

"Oh," the cart-wielding maniac giggled. "Those backpacks are so cute, but they can be such a pain sometimes!"

"Yeah," I agreed, flashing my gummiest, widest smile. "Though it generally isn't bothersome until someone tries to ram a cart up my ass. You can go ahead and try it, but I'd have to charge you my standard rate unless you have a military ID."

It was starting to get pretty hot in the store. At one of the registers, a couple was arguing with the cashier about a seven-foot fake Christmas tree that had been advertised but had sold out; at the other register, a woman who had gone to high school with Mary Todd Lincoln moved up to the counter with a wagon full of twenty-nine-cent gold and red silk flowers.

"Twenty-nine, twenty-nine, twenty-nine," the cashier announced as she scanned each tag.

"No!" the silk-flower woman crackled. "That one was from the twenty-five-cent cart!"

"I bet the last time you were behind a cart it was being pulled by oxen," I said under my breath.

"Twenty-nine, twenty-nine, twenty-nine . . ."

Suddenly, from the corner of my eye, I saw something suspicious, something miraculous. A man in a craft-store apron was moving slowly behind another register, and with his hairy hand, he reached over and flipped on his "open" light.

I don't think you could have gotten a bunch of women to move more quickly if someone had announced, "Oprah is giving away free cars on the glitter aisle, and she's paying for the tax this time!" Before I could even begin to move toward that line, however, the women behind me executed a cutoff and changed lanes without signaling.

The rat-haired woman and I gasped together.

"That's not fair!" she shouted. "Nine people behind us just got in that line! We were here first! He didn't take the next person in line!"

"The cashiers don't care," I said drolly. "The same thing happened the last time I was here."

"Really?" the rat-haired woman said as I nodded. Then she raised her little rat head above the crowd, shot the new cashier a dirty look, and yelled, "Hey, YOU! Cashier man! We were here first! You didn't even ask who was next in line!"

"What do you want me to do?" the cashier asked harshly. "Do you want me to stop helping this lady and help you instead?"

The rat woman thought for a moment and then looked him straight in the eye. "YES," she hissed. "YES I DO."

"Twenty-ni—"

A hush fell over the whole store and everyone just stared as the rat-haired woman made her way through the congestion to the front of the new line and plopped her stuff on the counter, never once dropping her head, never once unlocking her little red eyes from those of the cashier.

Sally Field couldn't have done it better. I felt like clapping and throwing long-stemmed roses at her.

"Forty dollars and sixty cents is NOT right!" the silk-flower lady yelled to her cashier, her shaky finger pointing. "I had it all figured out on paper this morning! You're trying to cheat me!"

The couple arguing with the cashier marched out of the store, the line moved forward, and the woman in front of me took her place at the checkout. Since she was purchasing only several boxes of string lights, the transaction was smooth, easy, and almost over.

"I will not be cheated!" the old silk-flower woman yelled. "We're going to count these together, and then you'll see what a cheat you are!"

The lady at the other checkout was signing her name to her check. It was almost over. Almost over if I could just hang on, although I could feel an attack of Mall Malice—Road Rage's bitter little sister—coming on, and I very badly wanted to pinch somebody.

"And here's your receipt," the cashier said, smiling pleasantly to the light lady in front of me. I took a step forward, anxious, waiting. I was drunk with anticipation.

"I want you to plug in these lights to see if they work," the lady said as she took the receipt.

I wasn't sure if I'd heard her right, but then she opened the package of lights and started fishing around for the cord.

I believe it was at this moment that I fell off the teeter-totter, that I lost whatever grasp I had on what was left of my patience, and my pinching fingers began twitching.

Naughty, naughty.

"NO WAY!" I heard myself freak out. "No way. NO. You are not plugging in those lights. You DO NOT get to do that." And then to the cashier, "She is not plugging in those lights." And to the crowd of angry women behind me, "She wants to plug in the lights!!"

"I don't have an outlet," the cashier offered.

"But I want to see if they work," the light woman insisted.

"I don't get to test out this stamp before I buy it!" I bellowed as I held up my item, then pointed to the woman behind me. "She doesn't get to try out her paint. Those are the rules."

The light woman just looked at me, holding the cord in her hand.

I stood there, holding my stamp in mine.

Naughty or nice.

I turned around, put the stamp down on the closest shelf, and walked out of the store.

Then I drove to another craft store clear across town.

As I was standing eighth in the checkout line with another

stamp in my hand, the cashier one register over flicked on her light and a thousand women guided by glue guns descended upon her like she was a naked grapevine wreath.

"That's not fair!" the woman behind me said. "She didn't take the next person in line!"

"The cashiers don't care," I said. "The same thing happened the last time I was at one of these stores."

O Holy Night, *or*
The Year I Ruined Christmas

When I saw my mother's new Christmas tree, I have to admit I didn't know what to say.

"Nice, huh?" my mother said, beaming and nodding toward her new holiday finery. "It's nice, right? I bet you've never seen another tree like it! It is a beautiful tree."

"It's something," I finally offered, wincing a little to protect my eyes from the shining glare of it. "It sure is bright."

"It's not *bright*," my mother clarified. "It's *festive*. There's a difference."

I didn't say anything.

"There *is* a difference," she tossed out before she walked away.

If that's the case, then my mother's new tree had more festivity than the searchlight from the police helicopter that hovers over my neighborhood on any given Friday or Saturday night and can turn night into day faster than God or science. Gone was our old, blinking-colored-lights tree, the fake tree that took hours to assemble and boasted branches with needles so realistic they drew as much blood as hypodermic ones. Gone were the yarn, macaroni, and pipe-cleaner ornaments my sisters and I had made as kids, coldly replaced by new decorations made by craftspeople—complete strangers—from colored clay and yarn, which served as evidence of my mother's recent trip to the Holy Trinity Craft Bazaar at her church (I knew Jesus was good with the water/wine thing, but you should see what that Savior can do with some Fimo clay and a garlic press). And that was not all. The new, fancy tree itself was not so much a tree as it was a miracle of fiber optics, for the tip of each "needle" on each branch glowed, turning from red to pink to purple to blue to green to yellow and then back to red again, the whole spectrum of the rainbow in a hearty luminescence.

"You bought a Gay Pride tree?" I asked my mother. "I am so impressed by your social progress, Mom! The next thing you know, we'll have you believing in evolution!"

"Call it what you want," my mother said, pretending to be nonplussed. "But I was just lucky to get it. In the last minute before the QVC clock ran out, all of those filthy vultures swooped in and this tree sold out with *four seconds to spare.* I have never seen anything like it, and I'm just lucky that I knew a good tree when I saw it and acted quickly!"

"Well, I guess the good news is that Chernobyl has found a new industry in selling glowing foliage that's been exposed to massive doses of radiation," I said. "Does it come with a lead suit of armor, or do you have to purchase that separately on QVC?"

My mother sneered. "Whatever," she replied. "I don't care if you like the tree or not. I LOVE the tree. I LOVE THIS TREE. I've just learned my lesson that if I want to touch the tree, it's best to unplug it and let it cool down first. I don't think my hand is blistered, but it's still stinging."

"Where's the gingerbread-house ornament I made in first grade?" I asked sternly as my squinted eyes searched through the branches. "And where are all of the candy canes Lisa made from pipe cleaners when she was in kindergarten?"

"Now that you're old enough to be a grandmother, I thought it was time that we moved on and had a Nice Tree without all of that crap on it," my mother said simply.

I blanched at her frostiness.

"Okay, yes, it's true," I snapped, "women my age are grand-mothers, but only in countries where people are swallowed whole on a regular basis by boa constrictors and a home invasion means there's a tiger on your kitchen table. In that same country, you'd be considered a witch for living longer than an elephant. And what do you mean by crap? Gingerbread houses and candy canes made by the hands of your little children are now *crap*?"

"I'll tell you what," my mother replied. "I'll give you the crumbling, disgusting, bug-infested gingerbread house and torn paper chains and bent-up pipe-cleaner candy canes you made, and you hang it on *your* tree."

"Hey!" I snipped. "You signed up for the motherhood cruise, my friend, not me. Hanging on to my childhood memories and all the stuff I don't want in my own house is part of that deal, you know! Now, why would I want my house to be covered in caveman paintings and have a tree that looks like it was decorated by little monkeys? I don't have kids for a variety of reasons, including not ever wanting to hear my name on CNN's *Headline News*, but certainly having a Nice Tree is a top contender. Nice Trees are a luxury reserved for childless people; we don't get the tax deduction and we'll spend our twilight years alone and getting our diapers changed by a high school dropout named Kenny in a nursing home, but while we're still able-bodied and selfish, we get prettier decorations and furniture with not as many stains. I'm a clear-lights person now, and the colored lights and the construction-paper ornaments are your responsibility. That's the balance. You're on my turf, MOM."

"I have wanted clear lights for a long time," my mother hissed. "I've always been a clear-lights person *inside*. It was you kids that wanted the mishmash of every color! I don't even have clear lights on this tree because of you! And balance? Do you really want to talk about balance? Because if you do, let's not forget The Year You Ruined Christmas. Let's talk about that, when the scale of motherhood was tipped so heavily it got knocked off the balance beam like a little hungry gymnast hit by a sandbag. I should have killed you that night myself!"

My mother loves to tell this story, because I think in her mind it really nails the point home to her audience that she has nothing less than Squeaky Fromme for a daughter and that I should have been incarcerated as a child.

Every Christmas Eve while I was still living at my parents' house, my friends and I would get together at a restaurant for a late-night dinner. The Year I Ruined Christmas was no different; my friend Doug picked me up, we went to another friend's apartment to have some drinks, and because I wasn't driving (see how responsible that is?), I may have had more than my fair share. Before I knew it, we were in the parking lot of the apartment complex, and everyone was splitting up and jumping in cars to form something of a caravan to go to the restaurant. I put my purse on top of the car and rifled through it to find a lighter for Doug, and then we were off.

We had a great time at dinner; we ate, laughed, drank some more, and had a wonderful Christmas Eve until the restaurant closed at midnight. When we went to pay the bill, I reached for my wallet, but it was difficult to find, being that my entire purse was gone. Although Doug, who had consumed enough alcohol to both kill and embalm him, accused me of being cheap and conveniently "losing my wallet," I knew well enough what had happened; I had left it on the roof of the car after looking for a lighter for him.

I wasn't really upset about losing my purse. I was a little loaded and I only had ten bucks to my name in there anyway. As soon as we paid the bill, we drove back to the apartment complex to try and find my purse, but it was no use, it was gone. What I was worried about, however, was that along with the purse I had lost my keys, and that meant that when I got home I was going to have to wake my parents up to let me in.

This was bad, particularly since it was very reminiscent of an occasion a couple of years before when I was a senior in high school and went to a party and I saw the guy I liked with another girl. Instead of getting revenge the way a normal girl would by forcing myself on his brother or best friend, I drank a half gallon of amateur screwdrivers, or whatever you call orange juice and gin. A whole Tupperware pitcherful. Didn't even get a glass. One minute I, a girl who had never even kissed a boy, remember saying to a friend, "He doesn't know what he is missing, because I am *good*! I am totally *good*! And I'm not just saying that because I'm drunk. 'Cause I'm not. God, you're blurry! Ha ha ha ha!" And the next thing I knew, I was being swept out like Scarlett O'Hara in the arms of my gay Rhett Butler, Doug, who carried me to his car, which I threw up in, took me to his house, and put me into a bed, which I threw up in, and waited for me to sober up before my curfew, being that it was only 8 P.M. and the sky still showed streaks of sunlight.

Needless to say, by midnight, I was still more hammered than a nail, which was unfortunate because I needed to go home. Doug, who somehow summoned up more courage than Joan or Melissa Rivers's plastic surgeon, threw me back into the car and drove me to my house. He then carried me to the side door and stood there, helpless, as I unfortunately regained consciousness and then, as any crazy drunk high school senior would do, decided to employ a bit of whimsy and kick the door repeatedly instead of finding my keys and simply unlocking it. That was when my mother appeared like a phantom out of the dark, sucked me into the house, and accused me of being on LSD, although anyone with a nose could smell that gin was the culprit, thanks to the vomit shampoo that was still in my hair. Therefore, every time I couldn't fit a key into a lock after dark, my mother, convinced she could sniff out drug use like she was a K-9 cop and I was the *Go Ask Alice* girl, would insist that I was under the influence of LSD, angel dust, PCP, speed, opium, peyote, or the reigning drug of terror she had seen a story about on 20/20 that week.

So on the Christmas Eve night I had lost my purse, I knew knocking on the door and waking my parents up would have no different results than it did when I was a kicky high school senior, except that I was being dropped off by a particularly friendly prelaw student who I just happened to be smitten with who had helped me in the unsuccessful hunt for my purse in the apartment-complex parking lot. I was really hoping my mother would cool her McGruff the Crime Dog bit long enough for me to seal the deal and get something more than a "Please stop driving past my house, you're scaring my mom" demand when he delivered me home, but when he walked me up to the side door, there was something I had hardly expected: a note from my mother.

"Laurie," it read. "We know that you don't have your keys, so knock when you get home. If you're still sober enough to read this, do NOT do your drunk dance on the door, and if you're on angel dust, the front window is not a liquid pane of glass as it may appear in your druggie state, so do not crash through it. You will be grounded."

I couldn't figure out how my mother knew that I had lost my keys, but as soon as the door opened, my best, glorious, magnificent, and totally bitchin' dreams came true. So much so that I didn't even care that my almost-suitor had bolted to his car and sped away after learning that I was apparently peaking on angel dust and may have been about to take a stroll through a plate-glass window, thinking it was a beautiful paradise waterfall.

Because inside my house was another sort of paradise just waiting to be revealed when my father opened the door.

Swinging from my mother's fingertips was my purse, the same purse that had slid off a car roof and landed in the parking lot of my friend's apartment complex. On that cold Christmas Eve night, after it fell off the car, it sat there for a while until a uniformed security guard making his rounds spotted the purse on the asphalt, saw the imprint of Doug's tire tracks over its belly, picked it up, opened it, and found my wallet and my driver's license with my address on it.

Ten minutes later, at my house, my mother had just sat down in the living room with a pack of Winstons and an ashtray and was watching the opening moments of *Cagney & Lacey* when the doorbell rang. She steadfastly ignored it, devoutly hoping that someone else had heard it, such as my father, who was watching *The Fall Guy* in the family room, or my sister Lisa, who was watching *Miami Vice* in her room, or my other sister, who was watching *Dynasty* in her room, and would rise to the obligation.

The happiness and solace of a family on the eve of the biggest family holiday was about to be shattered even more than if their oldest daughter was tripping the light fantastic on some illicit substance and then completely ruined Christmas by attempting to pass through an architectural feature of the house.

That was because, despite three doorbell rings with significant pauses in between, my mother finally ground out her cigarette and answered the door. There, to her annoyance and displeasure but certainly not to her surprise, my mother saw a police officer. A uniformed police officer, and in his hand was my driver's license. That, I'm sure, did not surprise her, either. I'm sure she thought I had been arrested for crashing through various windows around the neighborhood, trying desperately to find my real house while lost in the crazed, psychedelic fog of an After-School Special.

No, the shock came when my mother realized I was not handcuffed in the backseat of a cop car parked outside our house, glittering like a diamond covered in shattered glass and blowing air farts with my mouth on the window; rather, she saw a cop hold up a flattened purse with tire tracks imprinted on it, and she heard him say, "Laurie Notaro . . . run over . . ."

". . . run over . . ."

And in a flash, in a glorious, golden moment, I had suddenly died in a truly tragic incident on Christmas Eve, which was far more dramatic, sad, and utterly spectacular than any Death Fantasy I could have ever dreamt up. It was an incredibly impressive and breathtaking death, I had to admit, and I imagined my mother as she crumpled to the ground as if falling through a trapdoor and sobbed heavily as she took on her new role of "Grieving, Heartbroken Mother Who, She Realizes Now, Should Have Been Nicer and Kinder and Should Be Regretful About Being Thrifty and Making Sainted Daughter Buy Her Clothes at Kmart During Junior High School. Laurie Deserved Better, Namely, Casual Corner."

It was the gift that every girl dreams of, to be dead long enough for your parents to realize how meaningless their lives were without you, how they were suddenly and at once deeply sorrowed at all of the horrible injustices they caused you, how they had truly never appreciated your natural gifts of beauty and grace, and that they really should have bought you a nicer car, being that their beautiful angel would have such a short time on earth and should have spent that time driving the restored 1965 convertible Mustang she had openly AND PUBLICLY desired. But nope, she spent her last, short, fleeting moments driving a 1980 Chevy Citation, ever so clearly a GRANDMA car, with fake red-velvet upholstery, a hatchback, and an interior that smelled like spoiled milk and sometimes meat. Being temporarily run over by a car was the best present I had ever received, and I didn't even have to do anything dramatic to get it, like write a note or buy some rope.

It was indeed a holy night.

Then, unfortunately, my reverie was cut all too appallingly short when the "cop" stepped forward to inform her that it was only my purse that had become acquainted with several car tires, not the girl whose purse it was. He had merely wanted to return it.

"I was dead?" I asked my mother eagerly, trying hard to fight the urge to jump up and down in glee. "Oh my God. I can't believe it. This is fantastic! Did you cry?"

"Well, almost," my mother confessed. "But then again, there was the relief of getting a second use out of your prom dress."

Having me spend all of my eternity in black-and-hot-pink polyester taffeta would have been a grand revenge on my mother's part, and there was no doubt in my mind that she would have done it, too, although that skirt, complete with hoop, was so big the coffin would have had to be shrink-wrapped to keep it closed. No mind, I'm sure she would have voluntarily sat on it graveside before it was time to lower me down, as her friends looked on and sadly shook their heads at a mother who treasured her child so much she sat on the casket to be closer to her daughter, even if she was a miserable drug addict who ran around maniacally in a parking lot until she got bounced by a car, all because she was hopped up on dope.

"You didn't cry?" I asked again. "Are you sure?"

"Cry? When I found out you were alive, I wanted to kill you myself!" my mother said as she thrust my purse into my chest. "Well, that's it. You've ruined Christmas. When a cop shows up at your front door on Christmas Eve, that's it. Your holiday is shot."

"Wait," I said, shaking my head. "I'm confused. Did I ruin it by dying . . . or did I ruin it by living? Or maybe . . . I was just resurrected. Like you-know-who."

"That is not the point," my mother insisted. "And you just made God sad by even thinking that you were just like His only begotten son. A stranger saw me get all worked up because your purse got hit by a car. Not a person. *Just an accessory.* Look at that purse. I bet you got it at a thrift shop."

"I did," I said proudly. "It was a dollar. And by the way, it wasn't a cop, it was a guy in a windbreaker and a hat who took ten dollars out of my purse! Look. My wallet is empty. He stole my money!"

"Well, I am so glad I almost had a heart attack over a purse so cheap you couldn't buy it in Kmart!" my mother said. "I guess he deserved something for driving all the way over here. And you still ruined Christmas!"

I didn't care. It was the Best Christmas I Ever Had, even if my purse did bear the brunt of the tragedy by being pummeled by a Honda Civic and then mugged by the hero. My mom thought I was totally, truly dead for a few seconds, and that in itself was a gift so precious it couldn't be taken back. It was my favorite Christmas ever, and I'd do it again in a heartbeat if given the chance.

"Don't be so mad, Mom," I added, trying to console her. "I could always die next year."

Now, over a decade later, standing in front of her fiber-optic Rainbow Brite tree, my mother was giving me the same look she had the night I rose from the dead.

"I love this tree and I have paid my price as a mother for every Christmas that you have been alive," she declared. "*And dead.* I am done with Crap Trees. I wanted a Nice Tree, so I bought one. I have earned it. And I don't want to hear another thing about it."

"Mom, don't you understand?" I said in one last sneaky, underhanded attempt to get my way. "When you hang our weevil-eaten ornaments on the tree, that's how we know you love us!"

"Oh," my mother said without skipping a beat, "I guess four years of orthodonture to rein in your *Hee Haw* teeth wasn't enough, huh? You thought you were being sneaky by lying on your headgear chart when I was writing out those checks, but who paid the price after all? All of that money and all you got was Buck Owens's mouth. That's right; you make fun of my tree, I'll make fun of your overbite."

If that was how my mother responded when the word *love* was introduced into a situation, I was more than happy to bow out now before she saw fit to hurl me into her fancy new nuclear reactor of a Christmas tree and melt the skin on one whole side of my body.

On Christmas Eve several weeks later, we gathered in front of the fiber-optic tree and passed out presents.

"That is some tree," my sister noted, squinting while the needles slow-burned from an achingly glaring yellow into a forest-fire red, as did the sheen on our faces.

"At least someone appreciates it," my mother said as she tore into a giant QVC box. "If I had waited five more seconds, I wouldn't have gotten it. Everyone wanted this tree."

"Well, it's no wonder. It's a sauna and a tanning bed, with

branches for complete coverage. Did it come with welding goggles so that you could actually look at it without burning your retinas?" my sister laughed as she opened a wax candle in the shape of a mini pound cake from my mother. "That thing is more damaging than a partial eclipse."

"Look at you open those presents, Nicholas!" my mother said in a desperate and cheap attempt to divert attention from her emergency flare of a tree. "The wrapping paper is just falling off your gifts! You look so excited!"

"I'm sweaty," my nephew said as he wiped a line of perspiration from his forehead. "Your tree is hot, Grandma. My presents are getting soggy from my head."

"Come over here, we'll put some sunblock on you," my sister said as she ripped open wrapping paper to expose a wax cinnamon bun.

"I don't want to be an alarmist," I mentioned. "But if we're going to stay in this room, I think we'd better move the presents away from the tree. Having paper, cardboard, and batteries near that thing is simply inviting both danger and the fire department."

"LEAVE THE TREE ALONE!" my mother roared as she stopped opening her gift. "Why do you all want to ruin my Christmas? Isn't one ruined Christmas enough for a lifetime? All I wanted is a Nice Tree. I wanted to finally have a Nice Tree. What is wrong with that?"

"Nothing is wrong with it," my sister agreed. "You can have

a Nice Tree. I happen to have a Magnificent Tree. I have nothing but Lenox ornaments on it that I got at the outlet mall, and clear lights. Yes, that's right. I *said clear lights.* I've always known I was a clear-lights person and I'm tired of living a brightly colored lie."

My mother gasped. "What about the kids?" she cried. "What about all of the ornaments they made you this year? Nicholas made reindeer out of clay, and David molded his hand in plaster! Doesn't that mean anything to you?"

"You know," my sister replied. "I love my kids, but Nicholas is in the first grade. He brought home eight primitive clay formations that look like doody with legs. David has been sneaking into the living room and watching Will Ferrell movies after we go to bed, and in his plaster mold, he's clearly flipping the bird. Putting those things on my tree with a bunch of Cheerios ornaments and paper chains is simply not an option. My Magnificent Tree is magnificent for a reason."

"See?" my mother said as she shook her finger at me. "What did I say? Lisa agrees with me!"

"So I bought the kids their own tree," my sister finished. "And it's in the family room and it has all of their decorations on it. How could I not have our family tree? How else would they know that I love them and their legged reindeer poops and middle fingers? That's our family on that tree and in those ornaments; there's no way I'm going to leave them in boxes until they disintegrate."

My mother, perfectly stymied, sat there with nothing to say. After several seconds, when it was clear that even though she was out of the five-foot radius of the tree's hazard zone and that her face was still a little too shiny, she finally relented.

"Fine," she said as all of our faces turned from green to blue to purple. "Fine. Next year, I'll bring your ornaments back out, all right? But I'm not putting them on this tree, they would just be kindling, and Christmas trees should only catch fire if you live in a trailer. Anybody care if I unplug it? It's starting to make me nauseous."

My sister and I just smiled at each other as my mother, with a dish towel over her arm to prevent a major skin graft, pulled the plug out of the wall and the room turned dark, then dropped by 20 degrees.

There's a Gun Somewhere
Under the Christmas Tree

Right according to plan, the moment my poor future mother-in-law opened her front door, she looked at me as if she had just seen me slide down a brass pole and shake my bare hips to a Nazareth song as a fat biker rewarded me by sticking a buck in my thong.

It was absolutely horrible.

And I suppose she had every right. There I was with my bleached and pink and purple hair; what else did I expect? Certainly, I'm sure, she expressed a sigh of relief that I hadn't just been on the news for diddling the president or a congressman, so things could have been worse, but still. I was far from Julia Roberts, even as a hooker in *Pretty Woman*.

When the ghastly moment passed, my boyfriend's mother bravely put on her best smile and invited me in.

After all, it was Christmas Day.

Frankly, I just wanted to find the bathroom and stay there, and I probably would have, had my in-laws-to-be not thought that my absence was due to snorting a pound of cocaine rather than bone-chilling fear.

"I don't understand your friend's hair," I learned later that my boyfriend's sister said. "Why is it so many colors? And so unbrushed? I've only seen homeless people with that kind of hair."

"I used to have purple hair," my boyfriend reminded her. "And the knotty parts are just a couple of dreads; they're supposed to be there."

"Why is she wearing cowboy boots? Is she in the rodeo?" the other sister inquired.

"People wear combat boots who aren't in the army," my boyfriend reminded them.

"And this is the girl, Gloria, that you've been seeing?" they asked.

"No, this is the girl, Laurie, that I'm going to *marry*," he reminded them.

"Oh," they all said.

I really tried to put on a good show, to smile, to act pleasant, chew with my mouth closed, all of that stuff. I even retired the red lipstick for one day and switched to the Saucy Mauve that I had left over from my duty as my sister's bridesmaid.

In a kind maneuver to make me feel like I was part of the

family, my future mother-in-law took me upstairs and asked if I'd help her wrap some last-minute gifts, a duty I couldn't have been more grateful for. It would permit me a few minutes out of the spotlight, I thought as I wrapped and followed her instructions for which tags went on which presents, enough time for them to get used to me, and now maybe the children wouldn't cry or ask if I was a witch when they saw me come back down the stairs.

As I returned with the wrapped gifts, my boyfriend met me on the landing.

"This is horrible, they hate me," I told him as I handed over some of the presents. "I think I'd rather have my next Pap smear broadcast over satellite TV or have my credit report published in the paper or just about anything than go back in there."

"It's fine, it's really fine," he said. "They seemed to like you a whole lot more when I told them you weren't pregnant."

"Oh, good, good," I said, nodding my head. "They think I'm Courtney Love, don't they?"

"Listen, you're wearing a bra, aren't you?" he whispered. "Because somebody said something about maybe seeing a boob . . ."

"Yes!" I whispered back. "Of course I'm wearing a bra! You know we have to wear bras at the magazine because if we don't, the police surveillance team might mistake us for one of the porno people making movies in the office downstairs from us!"

"Just checking," he said. "Just checking. Keep your arms crossed, just in case. Okay, are you ready to open presents?"

"No," I answered honestly. "But I wasn't ready to be the boob-flashing rodeo witch that I apparently am, so let's just go."

The present-opening began, and with the paper tearing and the kids squealing, for a moment, everything seemed okay as I sat back with crossed arms and watched.

"Wow, thanks, Mom," my boyfriend said as he held up his gift. "A *Snow White* video!"

"Thanks, Mom!" his sister said excitedly, holding up a pair of pearl earrings. "They're beautiful!"

"Aren't . . . those the earrings I asked for?" his other sister stuttered.

"I didn't have this on my list, but I guess we could use it," her husband said as he poked at what looked like a nursing bra. "I know I've gained a couple of pounds, but do I really need it? Tell me honestly."

"If anyone unwraps a gun, I'm calling first dibs," my boyfriend's brother asserted.

Everyone looked very confused except for my future mother-in-law and me. I already knew what had happened, and against all odds, no matter how impossible it seemed, I had completely destroyed the family's holiday even further than I had when they thought I was a pregnant, homeless stripper with knotted hair.

In my haste, in my stress, in my panic, I had apparently stuck the wrong tags on the wrong gifts, damaging the gift exchange, and as a result, a three-year-old was handling a Leatherman tool with about eight different knives on it, two sisters were about to rumble under the Christmas tree, a gun was possibly in our midst, and it was suspected that a coveted Diaper Genie was hiding somewhere under a tag with the phantom Gloria's name on it.

"I'm so sorry," I professed over and over again. "I am so sorry. I don't know how this happened. I am really, really sorry."

It was then that my boyfriend's nephew, a frisky, one-year-old toddler, waddled up to me and immediately went straight to second base, making a far quicker move than his uncle ever did. I didn't know exactly what to do, so I just sat there, trying to smile as he grappled at my right boob and trying to pretend I didn't have a baby feeling me up.

"Oh, he must be hungry," his mother said as she laughed and pulled him off me.

"Wow," I said lightly. "I've never been mistaken for a snack bar before."

"Here," my boyfriend's brother-in-law said as he laughed

and tossed me his nursing bra. "I think this is probably for you."

They all laughed, and I laughed, too. When I looked at my boyfriend's mother, I saw that she was chuckling as well, and when she finally looked at me, she winked.

Have Yourself a
Kmart Little Christmas

Believe me, standing in line at 10:30 P.M. on Christmas Eve in a Super Kmart was not exactly how I planned to spend my holiday, but there I was, thinking that the only place I could be more tortured would be church with the rest of my family as my mother introduced me to her entire congregation as "This is the daughter I told you about who compared her fake death to the crucifixion of Jesus, which we all know after watching *The Passion of the Christ* was *not funny*. She's going to hell."

The Kmart by my Nana's house literally began to decompose after it had sat on a corner for twenty years, and then completely liquefied one night during a rainstorm. It was shoveled away and rebuilt into a Super Kmart, as if the landscape of a regular Kmart wasn't magnificent enough. It had to be supersized, despite the fact that the corporation was teetering on the verge of bankruptcy. There had to be more room made for bath towels you could see through and the universe's biggest selection of flammable clothing. The world simply demanded it. Frankly, I thought the message from God was loud and clear when the first Kmart melted, but apparently, the need to buy plywood furniture in the same place you pick up some bruised apples was deeply underestimated on my part.

Life in our town was about to see a jump in the quality of living now that you could buy a terrycloth romper for $5.99, take two steps and enjoy life a little more by munching down a chopped, pressed, and artificially colored ham sandwich that was only four for a dollar. Then, if luck was riding shotgun in your cart and the blue light was still a-flashin', you could buy a stack of Styrofoam plates with nothing but nickels, pennies, and some lint from your pockets.

Yeah, I'm being snotty, but anyone who spent their childhood dressed in Kmart Klothes knows exactly what I'm talking about, and speaking from that experience, I need to tell Kmart something (aside from "You better thank your lucky polyester asses that I never burst into flame while standing within a twelve-inch radius of a lethal toaster, waiting for a Pop-Tart"): If you want people to shop at your store, you don't need to make it bigger, you just need to STOP SELLING CRAP. Just stop. Resist the urge. I know it's hard. Terrycloth is great for wiping up a spilled drink but has no place on the body, cardboard dressers should only be purchased for kindling, and cubic-zirconium heart pendants should have been declared illegal years ago. I know you have the Martha Stewart name behind you, but come on, even Cher could only carry Sonny for so long, and this Cher's bunked in the Big House. And frankly, as long as we're following an honest theme here, even *her* stuff is crap. Ever sleep on a polyester sheet? You'll lose more weight in one hour wrapped in that than you will after five years in a Vietnamese prison.

It's all crap. Start selling underwear made from cotton and you can put that silly blue light away; stop building Kmarts that take up a whole street and melt with one good sprinkle. So, in the name of my snottiness, I made a solemn vow to myself that I would never set foot inside of it, no matter what the circumstances. I especially cemented my vow when I heard that the Super Kmart was open the week of Christmas every day until midnight, including Christmas Eve. I decided right then and there that if they cared so little about their employees as to make them work late into Christmas Eve, then they would never get a dime of my money. Super Kmart, in my opinion, Super Sucked.

And I really believed my oath, I truly did. Until Christmas Eve, when my nephews were opening their presents and suddenly I understood that I was also in the presence of an unseen visitor. I had an unscheduled, unannounced guest, one for whom I had no present but who had a present for me. It was My Special Friend, weeks ahead of schedule. It was nothing short of a Menstrual Ambush.

I did the only thing a girl in my position could do: I went to my mother for help.

"Oh, please," she scoffed with a huff. "I haven't slept in fourteen months, and when I wake up every morning, there are little piles of dust at the end of the bed that used to be my bones. I don't have hot flashes, I have slow burns. I spend all of my spare time in the freezer aisle at Safeway hovering over frozen vegetables. What the hell would make you think I would have a tampon in this house? And grab a place mat from the kitchen before you plop yourself down on anything; I just bought this furniture."

Unwrapping your presents while standing up can be a challenge, but it was easier than lying to two hysterical little boys who might have looked at a suspicious place mat and needed to be told that Aunt Laurie was not dying, she had only been shot in the ass earlier that day. After the festivities were over, I headed straight for Safeway to pick up some necessary supplies because there was no way I was going to carry around a place mat in my purse until December 26.

But as you've probably already guessed, Safeway was closed.

As was Fred Meyer.

As was Fry's.

As was Albertsons.

All dark and empty, their parking lots filled with nothing but painted stripes and speed bumps.

Now, I thought about stopping at a convenience mart, but frankly, I'm a little picky about where I get my toxic shock from, and if all they have in stock is some generic off-brand "Flo-tex" box, I'll stick with the place mat, thank you very much. Maybe I'm choosier than most, but I didn't know what situation was waiting for me tomorrow—the pendulum could swing from a "Gee, I'm as light as air and I am so comfortable that I could slap on an Olympic-issue leotard and do a cartwheel in front of sixty million viewers" or "I have an anvil for a uterus, and a maxi pad with the absorption rate of a feather bed wouldn't even do the job right now."

I knew where I had to go: that red-and-blue terrible beacon in the night. I had no other reasonable choice. If I had, I certainly would have taken it.

But there I was, crossing the threshold to everything that I hold unholy, Super Kmart. I understood as I moved from the darkness of the parking lot to the gaping, cavernous entrance—the gateway to the other side—that everything contained inside was indeed super. It was super big, super filthy, and had a more concentrated Super Kmart smell, which is a combination of equal parts popcorn, brand-new plastic, and baby poop.

Now, in the history of mankind, a store has never been as

crowded as Super Kmart was on that night. Almost every aisle was simply a river of people, as the wandering, mulling, drifting, roaming, itinerant mob of Super Kmarters swept the store. The only other time I've seen movement en masse like that is on the news when a country gets invaded. I was definitely the Grace Kelly in this store, but that's not saying a whole lot when people in prison looked like candidates for political office next to what was roaming around near midnight at Super Kmart.

In addition, chances were good to excellent that I was the only person in the whole joint who hadn't given birth earlier that day to the newborn slung over her shoulder, who actually had hair grown from her own scalp, who didn't have a lesion or open wound of some sort on or about the mouth area, and who was wearing shoes. It was like a whole different plane of existence. I wasn't even sure if most of the people in there were MAMMALS.

Somehow, I bodysurfed over to the feminine-hygiene department, caught several diseases, and ended up staring at a wall full of maxi pads. I needed variety, sure, but with this much to choose from, the selection process itself took on the proportions of a calculus problem. I had more trouble choosing a panty liner that night than I did a 401(k). The plain truth was I didn't know what I needed, and looking at all of the options just made me more confused. There was even a maxi pad shaped like a stealth bomber in case I was wearing a thong. Was the deodorant factor necessary, or was I willing to take the risk of a sudden breeze shooting toward my crotch? Just how many people would notice I had gone the extra-deodorant-tampon mile for them, anyway? "Wow, what a fresh breeze! Hey is that—Playtex Deodorized Tampons. Certainly. Thank you, Laurie, thank you, for your consideration and compassion toward others even in your time of suffering." Did I feel that my little friend had the desire to up the ante and push me into nighttime-protection territory? Did I need to fly on faith or buy the Leak Lock patented-technology maxi pad? Should I just scrap this whole expedition and simply get training pants? Did I think there might be a real chance for the expanded wing potential here? Not only were there wings, but then I spied Kotex Long Super Maxi with Wings and thought immediately, LONG? *Another variable?* How do I know if I'm *long*? I panicked. I had never even had the prerequisite curious moment in a bathroom and just happened to have a tape measure nearby to even come close to owning that nugget of knowledge. How does one suspect that one has a long cookie? Where is the chart? I've never seen a chart, not even in the nurse's office. What are you doing in your everyday life that would cause you to think, "Oh my God. I must have a long one. Nothing else makes sense." Excess back fat, wide ass, rubbing inner thighs, there are clues to those challenges, but *long ones?* Since, however, I'd never had a problem and never had to tuck anything under on a bike seat, I came to the conclusion that I had a regular short, Italian cookie just like I had a regular short, Italian body, considering genetics and all.

That was not the only revelation that reared its ugly head in the tampon aisle at Super Kmart, however. It was during this scrutiny that I noticed something odd: Every box of a Kotex-brand product bore a bright red dot at the tip of the X, nearly the size of a nickel.

Needless to say, I am not a barometer of sensitivity, but even I was shocked. That can't be what I think it is, I said to myself; maybe it's a printing error, or everyone at Kotex has toxic shock so they didn't notice the little red period on all of their boxes. Then I saw a small display flag with the words "Kotex fits. Period." punctuated by none other than the little red dot, and I knew it wasn't a mistake or a joke enacted by a stoner at the printing plant after his toke break. It was for real. I shook my head. Now, maybe I was making too much out of it but I thought it was quite odd. In fact, I think that whatever copywriter cooked this up had a skull packed full of deodorized cotton instead of gray matter—I mean, who wrote this ad, Beavis and Butt-Head? Or me? I mean, honestly, how much do you think Kimberly-Clark paid an ad agency to come up with something clever, only to have "Kotex fits. Period." pop up on an easel in a meeting? Somebody should have fired the bozo who was holding the pointer, or at least picked up a bagel from the snack platter on the conference table and pelted him in the head with it.

I mean, if "Kotex fits. Period." with little red dot floating through it made the cut what *didn't*?

"Kotex fits. Suck it up!"

"Kotex fits. Bloody well right!"

"Kotex fits. PMS (Pretty Messy Stuff)."

"Kotex fits. When you keep flowing, and flowing, and flowing . . ."

Or how about "Kotex fits. For those days when saying that mean birds pecked at your ass will psychologically scar your eight-year-old nephew and feed his already unnatural fear of winged creatures."

Frankly, I could not bring myself to encourage that sort of lazy nonsense, so I moved over to the Playtex section, which had no red period, no crimson tide, no erupting volcano printed across the front of its boxes, grabbed a variety box of tampons and a couple of packages of maxi pads (one long, just in case). I headed out to the main aisle, which only minutes before was full of people but was now mysteriously empty of human cargo. I took advantage of this sudden spaciousness and dipped down the candy aisle to grab a bag of Milky Way dark bars, then headed to the checkout lanes. Then I understood why the store aisles were so empty—it was because all fifty of the lanes were open and loaded with customers three and four deep. It had taken me so long to pick out tampons that Super Kmart was near closing time. I decided that the smart thing to do was wait it out, so out of mere curiosity, I wandered into the food section to see if Super Kmart was super enough to carry my favorite chocolate sorbet, which I always have a hard time finding. But there it was, so I grabbed three pints, just to stock up, and as I rounded the corner, I saw my mother's favorite cookies, Mallomars, created deliciously from marshmallows and chocolate, which are also very hard to find, so I stocked up on those as well.

Luck was with me, because as I approached the checkout lanes, I spotted one that only had two people in line, compared with the other lanes, which were now four and five people deep. I slid behind the second guy, who seemed a little jumpy, and released a giant tampon-and-chocolate mountain onto the conveyor belt.

The first lady in line was buying a Norelco razor. Just one Norelco razor. When the cashier asked her if she wanted to purchase the extended warranty, the lady paused for a moment and said, "I don't know. Tell me about it." This, apparently, was bad news for the man ahead of me, who balled his fist and punched the wall behind him. I wasn't exactly sure why he was mad, if he was in a hurry and didn't feel like standing there for eight minutes during the question-and-answer segment of the Norelco warranty spiel, or if the massive herpes sore that was eating away his upper lip was beginning to pain him. Either way, it was a delight to watch until he began kicking the wall of the checkout lane and uttering phrases in his native tongue that I didn't understand but wished I did, because I realized that I was in a Super Kmart, where anything can happen. If I had been at Target, my level of alarm wouldn't have risen nearly as rapidly, but at Super Kmart, you've got a careful, delicate balance, with a fingertip barely grazing the pulse of civilization, which can dip the wrong, volatile way at any moment. That happens when you've got a bunch of lunatics roaming around your store trying to buy vast quantities of Sudafed and acetone. In Target, you don't have to worry so much; Target sells cotton. Kmart sells gun cabinets. Recognizing this potential danger and the fact that apparently no one seemed to notice or care that the wall had been assaulted, much less stepped forward to do anything about it, I decided to get out of the way and took a couple of steps back, lest the Tasmanian Devil whip himself into a fury that somehow involved me and my skull. This, however, caused me to step on the foot of the teenage asshole waiting behind me with a cluster of his gangster homies.

It was just the sort of thing that I needed in order to call his attention toward me, as he and his friends began jousting back and forth in quieter tones, but what really got them going was when one of them called me "Peppermint Fatty." Which was nice. I always enjoy being judged from behind.

Even though I apologized for stepping on his foot with my gargantuan Peppermint Fatty hoof, I had become worthy of receiving not only his full wrath but the wrath of his hooligan friends as well. I'm guessing that they noticed what was heaped on the conveyor belt, because one of them asked another what time it was, to which the other replied (in a groan), "I don't have a watch, but it feels like my time of the month, man."

And with that green light, it all began.

"Hey man, how you feelin'?" one homie said to another.

"Oh, not so fresh, man, not so fresh!" a second homie answered, to which they all chortled.

"What stays in the dark, has wings, and sucks blood?" a third homie said.

They all snickered, but no one replied.

"A tampon!" answered the third homie, giving his own joke the wrong punch line, which was idiotic, because the correct answer was right there in plain sight on the conveyor belt, in long and unlong form.

"What do you do when a Kotex is on fire?" another one asked his stumped audience. "Tampon it!"

I stood there, frozen in an ice block of horror, hate, and bare naked humiliation. There was no way out, there was nowhere to go, I was in a realm of unimaginable mortification, and I actually looked down hopefully to see if I was naked and this was nothing but a bad dream brought on by deep-running insecurities and too much cheap wine.

Now, this exchange of period jokes continued for quite a while, and these are only the ones I can remember. After a while, the jokes weren't even about me anymore but had evolved into an odd adolescent-male ritual of trying to outgross one another, though I doubt that, in the history of mankind, a group of six fourteen- to seventeen-year-old boys had spent this much time talking about girls' periods and the collection of tools they employed. It was amazing to me to think that a battery of menstrual puns had been using quite a bit of storage space in each of the respective homies' brains, yet I had a feeling if you asked them what they learned in school that afternoon, their responses wouldn't be . . . well, quite so fresh.

Finally, when the lady who was buying the razor had heard all about the extended warranty and had all of her questions answered to her satisfaction and then decided she wasn't interested, the aggressive man in front of me stopped kicking the wall, mutilating every candy bar within his reach, finally got to pay for his Sudafed and valu-pack of generic batteries, and was on his way to celebrate what was, I'm sure, a very merry Crystal-methmas.

I, in turn, got to listen to several more treasured seconds of teenage boys telling each other how unfresh they were feeling, and after I paid for a year's supply of period products,

I grabbed my bags and turned and faced the Menstrual Gang.

"I got my period for Christmas," I said proudly to them. "And I'm glad you think it's so funny, but if I were you, I'd be hoping against hope that all of your little girlfriends got the very same thing."

Mashed Potatoes, Yams, and a Urine Sample

"**A**re you sure this is the one you want?" my husband asked, holding the trunk of a pine tree in a fenced-in portion of the Safeway parking lot.

Honestly, I wasn't. The tree looked quite lopsided, was bare on one side, and had the branches crushed in on the other. But I'm not a fool; I knew what I was up against. I had learned from Christmases past that if I didn't pick out a tree in forty-five seconds flat, my husband would start getting nervous and aggravated and would interrupt my tree picking to announce that we had to go home right away because he needed to use the bathroom.

I looked at him, his hands covered in yellow sap, his right leg beginning to twitch.

"My God, I love this tree!" I shouted. "We could look for a

whole three minutes and not find a tree as good as this one! I've never seen such a beautiful tree!"

"Pay the man," my husband said, dragging it toward the car. That he had already started to get worked up was not a good sign. We still had to get the tree home and put it up.

Sprawled like a corpse on our front porch, the tree patiently waited as my husband approached it with a buzzing circular saw to cut off several inches from the trunk. This was also not a good sign. I was pretty sure that I had broken the saw over the summer when I ignored the safety tips in the user's manual and used my concrete front steps as a makeshift sawhorse, leaving so many teeth in the concrete that it looked like a shark had attacked my house.

Before I could say anything, my husband moved in and sank the blade into the tree. The tree twitched and bobbed as the saw began to scream and the blade stuck. He held on tight, his teeth clenched. The tree shook violently until my husband stepped on it and tried to pull the saw out. After that, everything happened very quickly.

The next thing I saw was my husband covering one eye and screaming and the saw, now emitting plumes of smoke, tiredly spinning to a halt at his feet with a slow, grinding wheeze.

"That's it!" he yelled as he marched into the house to flush out the chunk of wood that had smacked him in the eye. "I hate Christmas! I hate Christmas! I hate Christmas!"

I didn't say anything. It's always best for me, in these situations, to cower on the floor, roll over on my back, and offer myself for sacrifice, whimpering slightly. But personally, as I rested my head against the dusty floorboards and noticed my best bra (only one underwire missing) beneath the couch, I thought to myself, How can you hate Christmas?

I've grown to enjoy our family holidays and even look forward to them, despite the fact that they now include medical procedures, as was demonstrated at Thanksgiving when my mother hauled a blood-pressure monitor to the dining room table and made all of us roll up our sleeves. "What do you want me to bring for Christmas?" I asked her then as she tightened the cuff hard enough around my arm that I lost feeling in my hand. "Mashed potatoes, yams, or just a urine sample?"

Still, I look forward to sitting around the dining room table with my family, reminiscing about holidays when we were kids. We talk about how we remember Christmas as cold and exciting, as my grandfather, Pop Pop, walked my sisters and me around the block on Christmas Eve so Santa could deliver our presents early, because, Pop Pop said, "My girls are special." We held his hand as we pointed to an airplane in the sky, and he would agree that it was Rudolph, coming to make the special stop at our house. Even after a traumatic fourth-grade episode when someone spilled the beans to me about Santa Claus, I still went on our walk with Pop Pop and didn't say a word when he spotted a 747 and said that it was almost time to go back to the house. The best part of Christmas was that walk, watching our breath turn cold on a chilly desert night, smelling Pop's tobacco as smoke drifted back from his pipe, and hearing him say as he nudged me with a wink, "I saw your mother filling up your stocking with underwear again. My daughter never listens to you."

I really miss that. Although he fought hard to try to live long enough to see his great-grandchild and namesake, Pop Pop died two days before Nicholas was born. As a family, we've tried to focus on what we've gained rather than what we've lost, evident by the mountains of wrapped toys under the tree with Nicholas's name on them. Without saying anything, we'll all know it should be Pop Pop who hands Nicholas his presents, helps him tear apart a stubbornly wrapped package, takes him on Christmas Eve walks. And we know that the ever present sense of loss really can't be filled with any number of gifts.

After our traditional dinner of antipasto this Christmas Eve, we'll bundle Nicholas and his brother, David, in their coats and little gloves, and before we head out the door for his first walk, I'll have to say, "Wait. Take everything off. Grandma says we all have to wee-wee first so her test will be ready when we get back."

Then we'll head out again, in what has become a new tradition in our family, except for the submission of body fluids. I'm hoping that I'll get to hold one of the boys' pudgy little hands, and that an airplane will pass low enough that my sisters and I can point to the sky and tell him that Rudolph comes early for special little boys.

I'm going to keep a pipe in my pocket, just in case.

Deck the Mall

Every family has forbidden words, words that with just a mention can evoke a wretched event, a terrible memory, or may do nothing more than conjure the thought of something simply so horrible that it's better to ignore it and never think about it at all. Every family has forbidden words or phrases that take on a "That of Which We Do Not Speak" eminence, for fear that a metaphorical monster will leap out of the woods and skin our goats alive if we, well, had any. Although the rules are well understood by all members of the family, every now and then someone lets one of these awful words sneak out, or uses it as a fraudulent distraction to get out of trouble at the dinner table.

For example, should my father boast once again for no apparent reason at the dinner table that he received a Christmas card from George and Laura Bush, to avoid a rather unpleasant retort from the Democrats sitting across from him and the positioning of a fork in a threatening manner, someone might just venture forth and say, "That is almost as appalling as HAM AND ORANGE SAUCE, Dad," which would make the conversation sputter and then fall into a sudden and just coma. Silence would reign as we all recount, one by one, the occasion on which my mother served ham for dinner in a delightful orange sauce with what looked like currants or raisins in it. It was dee-li-SHUS, and we gobbled it down like little piggies. When my mother finally sat down, we complimented her on the magnificent meal and added that raisins in the sauce were a great, inventive touch.

"I don't know what the hell you're talking about, there are no raisins in that sauce," she replied, then looked at the gravy boat full of floating raisinlike things in it.

"Oh, God," she said as she jumped up with the boat in her hands and ran to the kitchen, where she dumped the sauce— apparently a *Fear Factor*–style concoction, complete with a wide assortment of larvae—into the garbage disposal, then screamed, "How old is that cornstarch?"

Another That of Which We Do Not Speak expression comes courtesy of my younger sister, Lisa, who at the age of seven let past her lips one of the filthiest things any human on this earth has ever uttered, and which is known in the Notaro circle as "BARN DOOR." One night, as we were all sitting down to dinner, my father walked into the kitchen and we all saw that he had neglected to, shall we say, batten down his hatch. An easy mistake, one we've all made at one time or another—I happen to prefer making mine directly preceding a job interview. Sensing an opportunity to be a courteous and helpful daughter, my sister aggressively pointed to his open fly and squealed, "Daaad! Your barn door's open," an expression she had no doubt picked up in the unsavory world of the monkey-bar area of the school playground, then added, "And I can see your cow!"

This, of course, rendered my father helpless, reeling in the numb spiral of protective shock, as would any Catholic father who had a daughter who was openly talking about his cow, even if she was simply mimicking things she had heard dirty children who lived in the mobile-home park say, even if she hadn't the slightest idea of what a cow was, or even if his fly was only halfway down and you couldn't even see beyond the barn door, let alone the animals and their stables beyond it.

"Uhhhhhhh," my father stammered until my mother ran in front of him to block the unseen horror from our eyes as she shrilly shrieked at us, *"No one can see your cow! No one can see your cow! Keep eating your hot dogs! Keep your eyes on the hot dog! No one is looking at any cows!"*

But the most ominous That of Which We Do Not Speak goes far beyond my mother feeding her children bugs or my sister allegedly seeing our dad's livestock play peekaboo; this phrase will not only stun the family into unreserved silence, entirely aghast with implication, but it is enough to make people simply get up and *go home.*

It is so menacing that it doesn't even have a nickname; it just is. No one will dare bring it up, even if my dad were to announce that he had invited the Bushes over for Christmas dinner and the squinty one was taking my chair. Once it is uttered, typically by my unassuming Nana, it seems to take on physical dimensions and hangs in the air, and hangs and hangs and hangs like a storm cloud threatening to ruin a wedding. It looms heartily, unperturbed, until finally either the bravest soul or the one who owes my dad the most money will venture forth and sacrifice themselves to the terror known as "Nana Needs to Go Shopping."

If you know anything about taking an octogenarian anywhere outside of a familiar (and secured) environment, you know that it's one of the most challenging experiences you can have. Forget about sitting on a tropical island for thirty-nine days forging alliances and trying to kill your own food; dismiss on-the-air face-lifts, liposuction, and jaw implants. If television producers really want to put something bloodcurdling on the air, all they need to do is take an elderly person, hand them a shopping cart, and boom, *"Where Is the FiberCon? I Haven't Had a Bowel Movement in One, Two, Three, Four, Five Days, Young Man!"*: *Old People Shopping*—the scariest reality show in television history—would be born.

Now, it's not that I don't love my Nana, because I do, I love her *very, very, very* much. But upon crossing the threshold of a retail establishment, my beloved Nana takes on a form I don't even know. She instantaneously transforms into Chucky in Easy Spirit pumps, only much slower. Despite the fact that she occasionally loses her balance, she stoutly refuses to give up those pumps and fancies the shopping cart as a steadying device, as if it's bolted to the ground like a bike rack instead of being a precarious plastic basket perched on top of four wheels shooting off in different directions, but then again, how crazy can things get when you're going at such a pace that only a time-elapse camera can detect that you've even moved *at all*? I am not allowed to help steer or command the cart in any way; in fact, I am not allowed to even touch the cart. I have never been sure why. I initially thought it interfered with the fine tunings of Nana's inner compass, or that she feared I would suddenly push her to the ground and stage a coup, but recent events have brought me to a far different conclusion.

That's because, despite her supposed lack of physical agility, Nana gets "lost" on 90 percent of all shopping trips and tries her best to evade capture, like a zoo gorilla tasting her first moments of joyous freedom. The probability of finding her in the same spot where you dropped her off before you parked the car is a guaranteed zero, and once she is finally located in the store, your chances of keeping track of her aren't much better. Nana is nothing short of, politely speaking, a handful.

She's like a toddler, but one who won't respond to the store PA system calling her name unless the loudspeaker is approximately two inches from her left, good ear. One moment she's right next to you, studying a Roma tomato with more concentration than it requires to defuse a bomb, and the next thing you know, there she is in the bakery aisle, verbally attacking a sixteen-year-old stockboy: "Remember when you stopped carrying my bread in 1998? It was the best bread *ever made*. You ruined my life, you know! *Ruined my life.* BRING IT BACK."

Then you must contend with The List, which no one in my family has ever actually set eyes on, despite the fact that it sets the agenda for a major chunk of our lives. Nana keeps it firmly folded in the palm of her hand, bringing it out only to see what obscure item we will spend the next forty-five minutes hunting for. You have to have a special security clearance to view The List, and so far Nana hasn't granted it to anyone, not even my nephews, who are bribed with dollars and chocolate and sent on special missions to secure it.

Taking Nana shopping is a duty that no one in my family is eager to claim. Several weeks ago, when it was my turn to dissipate the black cloud, I have to admit that I was a little resentful because Nana and I were alone in her living room when the phrase was uttered, and usually you'd at least get some sad looks and pity from cowardly family members and condolence calls afterward. I got nothing. Just a cold, hard stare from Nana, her hands crossed in front of her as she looked and looked and looked at me for a long, long time. That old woman didn't flicker. She stood her ground like a Ukrainian demanding an election recount. "Sure," I heard myself remit weakly, "we can go shopping. If you need to. I didn't realize you were that hungry. Do you have any yarn? I'd like to tie our wrists together, or you can just make a list and I'll go get whatever you need . . ."

The gravity of the situation then deepened a bit, when Nana added a clause to the phrase and she shook her head: "Oh, no, I don't need to go to the store. I need to go to the *mall*." Then she tacked on—without a shred of mercy—"I need to do my Christmas shopping."

Now, if there's a thought more frightening than that of Nana in a store, it's Nana in a building *full of them*. This is in addition to the well-known fact that if you take Nana to the mall once, you'll be taking her to the mall again in a round-trip, because Nana returns everything. I swallowed hard and prayed for a sudden emergence of a stone in my kidney so that I could pass the shopping torch on to another relative while I suffered a softer, much quieter pain.

"I have a list," she added quietly, sliding a folded-up piece of white paper from her blouse cuff, showing only enough of it for proof, then carefully sliding it back again.

"How many names are on that list?" I dared to ask.

"*Everybody*," Nana whispered.

"Give me the list and we'll order everything on the Internet,"

I begged. "You won't even have to leave the house. Please. Just give me The List."

Nana wore a look of disgust on her face, as if I was trying to get to second base.

"Save yourself the trouble and buy yourself some chocolate with your dirty dollar," she snapped. "No one touches The List."

There were, unbelievably, some good aspects to taking Nana to the mall, particularly the nonexistence of shopping carts, her number-one tool for a clean escape. Even if she does manage to flee without a getaway cart, we always know where to find her, although sometimes we take our time and make a few pit stops before getting to the Easy Spirit store just to make her sweat a little.

Once we got inside the mall, since I had no access to The List, I asked Nana where she wanted to go first. She pulled out the folded paper from her sleeve cuff.

"The List says Aveda," Nana informed me, barely unfolding the piece of paper she held tightly to her body. "It's for your sister, and she wants some hair tonics."

I'm sure I visibly gasped. Aveda had been the scene of one of Nana's most infamous public outrages several years prior, when the poor unsuspecting salesgirl who had greeted Nana at the door only minutes before with a paper cup of soothing, aromatic complimentary tea, suddenly wanted to charge Nana twenty-four dollars for a tube of hand lotion and Nana, honestly speaking, nearly challenged her to a rumble.

"That's not my order," Nana snapped. "I only had one thing of lotion."

"And it's twenty-four dollars," the girl informed her.

"You are out of your MIND," Nana said, then slapped her open palm on the counter loudly. "Lotion that costs twenty-four dollars! At least do me a favor and show me the gun if you're going to *rob* me. Elizabeth Taylor's lotion isn't that much, and she's a *real* name brand! She's *Elizabeth Taylor*! I don't even know who Aveda is! I never even *heard* of her! Name a movie she was in. Your free tea was stupid, too. Elizabeth Taylor's lotion is *a very nice scent. Free tea!* I knew you were up to something!"

I learned a lesson that day, and so did my sister, who had to usher her children outside so they wouldn't have to witness their great-grandmother transform into Shannen Doherty girl-slapping the chick who'd boinked her husband in front of a video camera. That lesson was that at the grocery store, hardly anything is over five bucks, but at the mall, the only thing that's within Nana's price range is a stale pretzel with a side of processed cheese. Now, I know Nana was around during the 1970s because I saw her every day, but either she wasn't paying attention to the rate of inflation or she thought there was a lot of unwarranted chatter on the news about tires or rafts. Somehow, my Nana got frozen in a price ice cube, mainly because my Pop Pop did all of the shopping. Since the fabric of Nana's life is polyester, her clothes can't disintegrate and she never needs new ones, so mall shopping was never a real priority. Thus she kind of lost touch with, for example, the price of lotion. I really believe that Nana didn't yell at the salesgirl to be mean; I think she blew a gasket because she's put up with annoyances and irritations for eighty-seven years, which is a long time, was nice about it for almost a century, and reached a point where her niceness reserve ran dry. Then the high-priced lotion just pushed a button, you might say, and ever since then, Nana has not hesitated to speak her mind, which is good but can be considered a freak-out by onlookers and store managers. If Nana thinks you're trying to scam her, she'll tell you, and if she thinks you ruined her life by discontinuing Arnold's Thin bread, she'll let you know that, too. I guess when you spend eighty-seven years swallowing other people's bullshit, there comes a time when you gotta spit some back. So that can take us on one of two routes: either we can spend a lot of time at the mall fighting with high-school-senior sales associates about why Sears is trying to con Nana over a pair of overpriced Dearfoams terrycloth slippers for forty dollars, or we can make our shopping experience relatively calm and security-guard-free by performing some preemptive measures.

Upon entering the store, we were approached by the salesgirl with the tray of paper cups, whom Nana brushed aside with her hand and the words "Save the tea, you're not sucking me into your lotion scam. I found out who Aveda was, and she wasn't an actress! She was just some bimbo who married the king of Argentina and they made a movie about her *that she wasn't even in.*"

Knowing that the chances of getting my hands on The List were nil, I asked Nana to read what she needed to get for my sister so I could help her find it. After she rattled off three items and we found them, I set my plan into action, grabbing some other things off the shelf and essentially throwing my credit card at the salesgirl.

"What are you doing?" Nana yelled. "Those are my things!"

"It's easier to put it all on one bill," I said, using the trust my Nana so devoutly put into me and twisting it like a dirty pair of undies in the wash. "When we get home, we'll figure it all out."

With that success under our belt, we, as dictated by The List, moved on to Eddie Bauer, where I tossed the two sweaters Nana had picked out for my husband and brother-in-law onto the counter with my Visa and signed away while she protested.

"Don't worry," I lied to the last person on earth who thought I had a hint of good in me. "You can just write me one check and we'll be even. How easy is that?"

We did this for the remainder of the morning, even at Banana Republic when I picked out a pretty sweater for myself that wasn't even on the sale rack. Shopping with Nana had never been easier. There was no haggling, no open-hand slapping, and no movie trivia involved.

It was absolutely amazing how simple it was, and I cursed myself for not thinking of such an obvious plan sooner. When we got to Nana's house, I took all of the receipts from my wallet and held them tightly in my hand.

"Now," I said to Nana, who had a pen in her hand and her checkbook open, "let's make this fun! I'm going to name a store that we were at today, and you guess how much that stuff was, okay?"

"Like The Price Is Right?" Nana asked.

"Exactly," I answered. "The first store is Aveda. How much do you think the stuff for Lisa cost?"

"Thirty dollars," Nana said firmly.

"That's incredible! You're exactly right!" I exclaimed, thinking that taking a forty-dollar hit was way cheaper than bailing Nana out of jail on an assault-and-battery charge. "Our next store is Eddie Bauer."

"Um, let me think," Nana said as she pondered. "For two sweaters? Hmmm. I say thirty dollars!"

"You must be psychic!" I squealed, thinking that I really didn't mind contributing an additional ten bucks per garment to be able to shop at Eddie Bauer again. "Now we're up to Banana Republic. Nana, give it your best shot!"

"THIRTY DOLLARS!" she yelled with a little jump.

"No, not quite," I smiled, reminding myself that this little ditty had come from the full-price table, and well, after all, it was for *me*. "Try again!"

Nana paused for a long moment, and then finally her eyes lit up. "I know," she said sneakily. "Thirty-one!"

"Let's take a leap of faith on this one," I said. "Aim higher, Nana! I know you can do it!"

"If that sweater is over thirty-two dollars, we're going back to the mall right now to return it," Nana informed me.

"Thirty-two dollars!" I cried. "I knew you could do it!"

"Let me see those receipts," she demanded, holding her little Nana hand out. "I think it's weird I guessed right on all three. I think something fishy is going on here."

Sure, it was true that I had tricked an eighty-seven-year-old lady like I was an executive at Enron, and I had subsidized Nana's shopping like she was a farmer in Kansas, but I was willing to pay the price to get it done. Done quickly and quietly. If I handed over those receipts, I might as well have gotten my car keys out, too, because that meant we were going back to the mall to undo everything we had just accomplished. *Everything.* It was a thought I simply could not bear.

"I'll make you a deal," I offered. "I'll give you these receipts if you agree that the next time we go shopping, I get to hold The List."

Nana fell silent and began writing out the check. I smiled.

A couple of weeks later, my sister Lisa called.

"I took Nana shopping today," she said as soon as I answered the phone, obviously looking for sympathy.

"Oh," I replied, mainly because I was still resentful that I hadn't gotten my fair and well-earned share of pity.

"AT THE MALL," she said for effect.

I choked on my own spit. "Was she trying to return things without receipts?" I asked. "If she returned a sweater to Banana Republic, I am charging her full price next Christmas!"

"No," my sister answered to my great relief. "But she made me take her to Nordstrom's to get perfume for Mom."

"Oh big deal," I pooh-poohed. "I took her all over that mall, including Aveda!"

"Yeah? Poor you. Well, I am willing to bet that no one had a heart attack on *your* shopping trip," my sister shot back.

"Okay, you got me," I said immediately. "I'm listening."

Apparently, Nana's list had been incomplete when I took her shopping, so my sister volunteered to take her, primarily because my dad had just bought her a car and the layer of obligation on that car was still pretty thick. Out to the mall they went, to the only store that carries the kind of perfume my mother wanted.

Once they got to the perfume counter, a nice saleslady helped them, found the perfume, and even informed Nana that it was a better deal if she purchased the gift set as opposed to the individual perfume. It even came in a box that was wrapped, although this posed a bit of a problem, since the computer code for the gift set was covered up, naturally, with wrapping paper.

While the saleslady was looking for the code in the big code book, the phone rang, and after she answered it, she told my sister and Nana that she had a family emergency and she would get someone else to help them. Nana allegedly wasn't very happy about that and said very loudly to Lisa, "THAT is the problem with service today. NO ONE wants to help you!"

That was about two seconds before the saleslady yelled to a co-worker at another counter, "Can you please help these ladies? My husband is having a heart attack and I have to go!" Then she left, running.

Unfortunately, none of this information reached Nana's good ear. All she saw was her saleslady running away, away, away, and not coming back.

Nana started tapping her hand against the glass, and by the time a salesman came to her aid, my sister firmly believed she was seconds away from an open-handed counter slap. He searched through the computer-code book and finally found it, seconds before my sister was ready to rip the wrapping paper off of the gift set herself to find the price.

"Okay, the perfume-and-lotion set is fifty-five dollars," the salesman said to them.

"Oh, *come on*," Nana scoffed. "THAT is ridiculous. You really expect me to pay that for some lotion and perfume? What is it with the lotion these days? Is lotion going extinct? You know,

Elizabeth Taylor's lotion is not that expensive, and it's *a very nice scent!*"

Sensing danger, my sister immediately went into action.

"You know what?" she said as she cleared her throat, got the salesguy's attention, and tapped her fingernail on the glass. "I could have sworn this set was on sale. I'm sure of it. Yes, this set was definitely on sale."

The salesman took my sister's cue, nodded, and wholeheartedly agreed as Lisa slipped a twenty into his palm.

"This set is twenty dollars off! It most certainly is!" he said excitedly, which calmed Nana down a bit.

"All right then, that's more like it," she exhaled with a deep breath. "Thanks to the sharp eyes of my granddaughter, I got a fair deal. What is it with you salespeople, always trying to rob me? Do I have a sign that says 'sucker' on my head? I should report you!"

"No one is reporting anybody," my sister said firmly. "It's Christmastime, and we should all be thankful that we're not the ones having heart attacks right now and that we all just have high blood pressure. Write out the check for the gift set, Nana. It's time to go home."

Back in the car, Nana took a deep breath.

"That was some day, huh? All that excitement," she said.

"Yep," my sister replied.

"Sure was different than the way I thought I was going to spend the day," Nana continued.

"Yeah? How was that?" Lisa asked.

"Oh, the usual," Nana concluded. "Sitting in the chair and moaning."

"Yeah, shopping sure beats that," my sister agreed.

"But I sure didn't expect to spend that much money," Nana said, shaking her head.

"Oh, me neither," my sister agreed. "But I think you made out like a bandit."

Jingle Hell

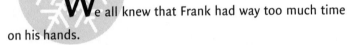

We all knew that Frank had way too much time on his hands.

All of the neighbors agreed, perhaps not in a ballot-casted community vote, but at one time or another everyone on the block had taken notice, assessed the situation, and had decided that the ninety-pound man who lived across the street from me had spun madly out of control.

It was far beyond *our* control, anyway.

The first indication that something was seriously wrong on our street came on Thanksgiving Day several years ago, in the shape of eight full-size plywood reindeer, complete with leather reins and bold, brass jingle bells, all planted firmly in Frank's yard. Behind them glided a robust, gleaming Santa and his sleigh, which was bigger than any actual car that the neighbors owned.

My neighbor Mike sadly shook his head as he scratched his belly. "That's a man with trouble in his heart," he said to me, nodding at the holiday extravaganza across the street. "And trouble in his pants. Somebody in that house needs to get laid."

I had to agree. We all knew Frank didn't have any kids and spent almost all of his spare time manicuring his already perfect lawn, which made the rest of the neighbors look really bad, especially because we had all moved into a white trash neighborhood specifically so we could spend our leisure time getting drunk and not installing sprinkler systems. Frank had no right trying to fancy up his yard; he was ruining our street, particularly when my next-door neighbors caught the Fancy Yard Fever from Frank and tried to gussy up their place during Christmas, too. The only problem with their improvement was that they were really poor, so they made all of their decorations out of used, broken things. The most precious of which consisted of a huge five-pointed star made out of silver tinsel, held up on an easel and framed with a circle of tinsel around the outside. In short, they weren't too bright, since they had inadvertently propped up an enormous, shiny pentagram six feet from my house in a very sorry attempt to outdo Frank.

The next year was even worse. In addition to the Santa setup,

Frank presented the street with a miniature Disneyland theme, including a Bambi, Thumper, all seven Dwarfs, and a terribly disfigured Dumbo that looked more like a sow than a circus elephant, which he nailed to the top of the tallest tree in his yard. That was also the year he set up a sound apparatus that blared out the Chipmunks and a twinkle-light system that required the expertise of an architect. It had become horribly apparent to all of us that Frank had redirected most, if not all, of his sexual energy away from his wife and into the direction of a jigsaw and sheets of lumber.

This was confirmed one afternoon when all of the neighbors came out to fake work on their yards so we could watch Frank fight with his wife as they were stringing up the lights and disaster struck. Frank's wife, it seemed, had handed him the wrong end of the extension cord, and in a fit of unleashed fury, he hurled it off the ladder and onto the ground, where it landed in front of her. She looked at the cord, then at him, and back to the cord again.

"Well, you can take that cord and plug it straight into your ass, Frank" was the only thing she said before she walked into the house. Frank got very nervous and started uttering mumbled phrases, although I did catch his comment that she "was only a woman, how could she know about man's work like this?"

On the heels of every disaster, tragedy naturally follows, and Frank's yard was no exception. One sunny December morning, everyone on my street woke up to Frank howling mournfully, and a brush of my bedroom curtains revealed a tortured man with his hands on his head, screaming for God over and over again in a crucial plea for compensation. A further brush revealed a handcrafted and diligently loved set of reindeer now embellished overnight, by way of black spray paint, with a full set of impressive male genitalia.

That night, the Chipmunks did not sing. Frank had a plan to catch the reindeer marauders. I don't know what it was, but I know that it included a tennis racket and a bunch of rope, because that was what he hauled out into the carport as the sun was setting. When it got dark, he commandeered his post in a corner of the carport, sitting on a wooden stool with all of the lights off, a little man alone. I couldn't see him but I knew he was there because I could see the glow of his cigarette every time he took a drag. The Christmas King guarded his castle for six nights in a row until Christmas came, and he never caught anybody.

The years that followed brought the "Peanuts" characters to Frank's house, as well as the Simpsons, Frosty the Snowman, and an assorted gang of demonic elves that guarded the compound with steaming red eyes not unlike those of Jody, the demonic pig from The Amityville Horror.

An attempt to kidnap Snoopy was thwarted when one of Frank's stepsons came home drunk one night and grazed several of the vandals with his car as he attempted to turn into the driveway, although they still managed to escape. This time, a tennis racket wasn't going to be enough security for the yard, and Frank unabashedly and almost proudly told me of the network he had set up in the neighborhood. It included other seasonal-decoration fanatics, CB radios, and guns. One guy was set up three blocks to the west and the other guy one block to the east. If a vandal was spotted, or even suspected, the network participants would signal to one another as to which direction the perp was heading, and if one was caught, Frank told me point-blank that he wouldn't hesitate to shoot.

The duration of that season, quite thankfully, was uneventful.

The next year, we could all tell that something big was brewing in the elf factory of Frank's backyard when sounds of saws, hammers, and sanders consumed our street for weeks. We held our breath for Thanksgiving Day, Frank's annual self-appointed unveiling date.

And we waited.

And waited.

And waited.

Thanksgiving Day came and went, blanketed with a bitter silence as our turkeys turned rancid.

Nothing was happening in Frank's yard, not a string of lights or a note of Christmas melodies. Something was very, very wrong. It felt dangerous.

It was impossible that he had had sex. His wife had left him during the summer.

Then, one night, I was napping when I heard it.

Tap tap tap.

Tap tap tap.

The tinkle of Frank's hammer.

I jumped out of bed, as I'm sure my neighbors did, and peered across the way to Frank's yard, but it was too dark. The sun had already gone down, and all I could see was a big, lumpy shape of something with a floating red light toward the bottom that must have been Frank. I was going to have to wait until morning. Frank, you see, was teasing us.

The next morning, the first thing I did, without even lighting a cigarette, was open the bedroom curtains to see the new creation.

It was bigger than anything I had ever seen on Frank's lawn before.

It was six feet tall.

It was a monolith.

It was wearing a Santa suit.

It was purple.

It was BARNEY.

Of course I screamed. The first thing I thought was that at nighttime, the thing was going to come alive, gallop across the street, and peek in my windows, mouthing that it loved me.

If Barney was the agent of Satan, as I believed him to be, that made Frank the devil, even if he did weigh less than me. My fear grew even more enormous when I remembered that I was having a Christmas party in a week, and if I knew my friends like I thought I did, Barney had better brush up on some tricks from hell or borrow my neighbor's pentagram for protection, because he didn't stand a chance against my guests, which, in turn, was going to put me in an ocean of boiling water with Frank.

Then a miracle happened.

Barney was shanghaied the night before my party. I couldn't believe my good luck. I was off the hook; I couldn't be implicated in Barney's abduction no matter what.

The night of my party, Frank hadn't even flickered the Christmas lights. The yard remained dark, black, and mourning.

My husband, under the influence of some foul though potent wassail, took a tribe of guests to the other side of the street to prove to them that I don't make this shit up. There they were, gawking and amazed at the finery, wondering aloud what kind of nut would put forth such a worthless effort, when a voice rang out from Frank's porch.

"GET OUTTA MY YARD."

They were in trouble. My husband knows that Frank has guns.

"We were just admiring your yard," he said. "How did you get rid of—I mean, what happened to the Barney?"

"WOULDN'T GET ANY CLOSER IF I WERE YOU," Frank warned. "I GOT TWO HUNDRED AND TWENTY VOLTS IN THIS YARD."

And he did.

The entire yard was laced with trip wire, starting at the Snoopy that Frank had placed in Barney's spot as a lure for when the bandits came back. The lawn, the Bambi, the Linus, the Bart, the elves, were as hot as the Chair when the switch is pulled—well, maybe not that hot, but pretty hot, hot enough to fry a little kid who could wander into Frank's Christmas Death Trap by mistake.

The boys got out of the yard and came straight back to the party.

The next day, I had to go over to Frank's to apologize for something else that happened that night. My friend Keith thought it would be fun to bring the British punk band, U.K. Subs, to my house, but by the time they got there, everyone had already gone home. The band didn't have anyone to entertain them, so they went outside and threw grapefruits at Frank's yard until Frank announced that he had his rifle cocked and that they were just moving targets to him.

"I probably would have just shot 'em in the legs," Frank assured me. "Good thing for them that they didn't come in this yard. Got enough volts running through here to knock a horse on its ass."

It was then that I noticed the newest addition to Frank's

yard, a handcrafted sign that was spiked right near the entryway.

FORGET THE DOG, it pronounced.

That was odd, I thought. Forget the dog?

Forget the dog?

Then it all made sense.

I read the next line.

BEWARE OF THE OWNER.

Well.

Enough said.

Where Do Good Trees
Go When They Die?

I had just finished opening my last present on Christmas Day when my mother asked me when I was going to take my Christmas tree down.

"I just finished putting it up today," I answered. "Finally, procrastination has rewards bigger and better than Discover card! Did you know that if you wait to literally the last minute, you get a free tree? The lot was deserted and the gate was open, almost as if the tree warden expected the leftover trees to escape. It was kind of like if it was the last episode of *Hogan's Heroes*."

"You can't let those things dry out too much," she said, ignoring me. "And with all the trash you have around that house, a fire will rip through it like a mobile home."

"I'll take it down soon," I stressed, trying to quiet her.

"You'd better," I heard her whisper.

The week after Christmas, little birdie chirps floated through the air, a cool yet gentle breeze rustled the leaves of the trees, and buttery sunlight glided through my bedroom window. I smiled when I woke up. It was a perfect morning.

Then the doorbell shattered everything.

Ding dong.

Ding dong.

Ding dong!

No one rings my doorbell in the morning like my mother.

"Hi, Mom," I said as I opened the door.

"Yeah. Listen," she nodded as she handed over a newspaper that had clearly been delivered to me by mistake. "I was just driving by and I noticed that you haven't picked up the newspapers in your driveway. You're just inviting someone to come in and rob you."

"Good morning," I smiled.

She looked past me. "Oh my God, that tree is still up? What, are you crazy? I'm telling you, it's a fire hazard. You are begging this house to catch on fire. When are you going to take it down? I smell smoke. Is that smoke?"

"Trees do not spontaneously combust, Mom," I said, dropping the papers into the recycling bin. "They don't all of a sudden catch fire for no reason."

"They do so," she quipped. "Why do you think I have a fake tree? They just melt when something goes wrong. A lady at church told me her neighbor's Christmas tree burned right down and took her La-Z-Boy with it."

"If this was the same church person who said she found a hooker's body in the bedsprings in the room where they were staying at the Excalibur, I told you not to listen to her anymore," I informed her. "It's an urban legend and she's getting that stuff from the Internet. It's not true, it never happened. Call the Excalibur to see for yourself."

"Why would she lie?" my mother insisted. "Why would you lie about a dead hooker in your room?"

"I'll take it down soon," I obliged.

"You'd better," she whispered, and then she pointed. "You really should wear a bra to bed, you know. Eight hours of extra support would go a long way."

I knew right then and there that I had been marked and a battle had begun. I was now, against my will and better judgment, locked in, and there was no way out. You see, my mother has an extraordinary talent.

She worries. My mother is the supreme agonizer. The woman is peerless. When she first heard the song "Don't Worry, Be Happy," she scoffed, nearly laughing, and said, " *'Don't worry'*? What a stupid thing to say. *'Don't worry'!* How else are you supposed to know you're alive?" However, as much as she enjoys the sport, she doesn't like to worry alone. Just as she is in charge of her prayer chain at church, she uses that same technology as a strategy in the war against her victim. She likes to organize a worry party and has been known to include other people in the worrying. We call this tactic the Notaro Worry Chain.

For example, she called me not too long ago in a huff and said, "You know your sister's damn dog? Well, it peed on the carpet. The stain is still there. You can't get it up. She tried *everything*. She's never going to be able to sell that house now. *Never*."

"But . . ." I said after a lengthy pause, "she's not moving. The house isn't for sale."

"She's not going to live in that house for forever," my mother immediately informed me. "People don't live in houses for forever. Not anymore. People are nomadic now, it's the trend. And when the time comes, well, there's that stain. Who's going to want a house with a stained carpet? I wouldn't buy a house with a dirty carpet."

Now, my sister's carpet wasn't dirty, and you could barely, barely, barely recognize the outlines of the stain, and that was if you were standing in great light. Nevertheless, every time my mother went to my sister's house, she stood above that stain and shook her head. "Never going to sell this house," she'd say to herself. "People will take one look at that and walk right back out the door, unless it's a dirty family. God, I will pray for a dirty family."

My mother lamented about the stain like it was a son off to

war in a foreign country. The stain haunted her. In turn, she haunted my sister until she hired a carpet cleaner and her house once again became sellable.

Now, I suppose I could have taken the Christmas tree down. It could have been that easy, except for one simple thing: I had vengeance on my mind and a score to settle. Earlier in the year, I had been the object of a Worry Chain maneuver escalated to a higher Worry level, a Worry Mission, when I had gone to New York, and as soon as my plane landed, the terror-alert level jumped to orange, which is typical and always happens. The moment I leave my state, the terror-alert level will jump a couple of rainbow steps; it's a given and I've learned to accept it. Either I have fantastically bad traveling luck, or I'm the terrorist, and either way there are a lot of extra hands on me probing into fat rolls when my barrette triggers the metal detector. I hadn't even gotten to my hotel yet when my mother called and demanded that I come home. "And I mean *now*," she said sternly. "The newspeople said you should have extra water and duct tape on hand for when the terrorists strike, which looks like it's going to be Tuesday at around three, isn't that what Fox said? Yes, your father said that's what Fox said. They'll probably stop room service at the hotel and your chances of getting a clean towel are just as slim. Come home now."

When I refused, my mother became indignant and went into full-force Notaro Worry Mission action. As soon as I got to the hotel, there was a message from Nana at the front desk that read, "Laurie? Is that you? Laurie? Stay inside tomorrow at three o'clock and ask for towels now."

As soon as I walked into the room, the hotel phone rang. I hesitated when answering it but thought it might be one of my friends that I was there to see.

When I picked up the phone, I realized how wrong I was.

There, on the other end, was my seven-year-old nephew, Nicholas. I love this child more than anything. He is my godson, and I adore him. My mother knows this.

"Aunt Laurie," my nephew said in between full-throated sobs, "please come home. Grandma says you're going to die tomorrow in New York when you're out having fun with your friends. Please don't die!"

Talk about a dirty bomb.

"Nick," I said as calmly as possible, "I'm not going to die. I will come home soon, and I promise I am safe. There is nothing for you to worry about. If I thought I might get hurt, I would come home, but everything is fine. Make Grandma get you an aspirin and then put her on the phone."

"What?" my mother said.

"You know what," I replied. "Why are you scaring a little kid?"

"Has anyone given you duct tape yet or a bottle of water? They're putting security guards at all the doors to the hotels, you know."

"They are not!" I cried. "I'm in a hotel! There are no guards at the front door!"

"Well, they are at the nice ones," my mother replied.

"Some words of advice, Ma," I started. "You're twenty miles from a nuclear-energy plant with THREE REACTORS, the largest one in the country. It's a big target in the middle of the desert and is kind of hard to miss. Duct tape and a bottle of water isn't going to stop your organs from turning to jelly with radiation poisoning, but maybe the tape will help when your skin starts slipping off like a drunk girl's dress. Worry about that, Ma, okay? Worry about that. And stop scaring little kids!"

True, when I finally got home safe and sound a week later, I got a hug and a kiss from a seven-year-old, which was nice, since the hugs had stopped with his acquisition of a Game Boy some time earlier. Nevertheless, my mother had violated the rules of the Worry Mission by employing child warriors on her behalf, and I was still pretty mad about that.

The Christmas tree was staying up.

By mid-January, the "That Christmas Tree Is Going to Kill You Situation" had naturally become a staple in our conversations, falling into place right after "Did you pay that traffic ticket yet, because I'm not going to be the one to drive you to court when your license gets suspended?" and before "Did you call the doctor's office to reschedule your Pap smear, because I don't want to be the one to drive you to chemotherapy when you get cervical cancer?" She didn't hesitate to tell me that she had lost sleep over the Christmas tree on more than one occasion and had dreams that presents under a Christmas tree were exploding like firecrackers and she had to spit on all of the little fires to put them out.

"One spark is all it takes," she added. "I wouldn't even *walk* by that room with a book of matches or a hot dish if I were you."

"So funny you should say that," I added. "It looked like the Christmas tree was actually smoking yesterday, but it turns out the smoke was from the cheap candle I had put on the table right next to it. And I think I'm going to start drinking and smoking again. I love being drunk and dancing with a cigarette in my hand!"

A week later, she called with a hot tip: "Kmart has fire extinguishers on sale. I'd get a couple if I were you."

"Oh, we already have one," I told her. "Although I lost the little booklet that says how it works. Well, if I see flames, I guess instinct will kick in and I'll figure it out. Guess what I'm wearing? Nylon pajamas from Kmart!"

By Valentine's Day, it was clear she'd been working the phones.

"Laurie? Are you there? Laurie?" called Nana's message on my answering machine. "God, I hope you're not not answering the phone because you're dead. Oh, I hope that tree didn't kill you! I will be so mad! That damn tree! Laurie? Hello? Laurie?"

Then my sister called. "Please keep the tree up for as long as possible," she pleaded. "My dog peed on the rug again."

The tree was driving my mother insane, and frankly, I was enjoying every minute of it. Actually, our Christmas relic had become so much of a normal part of the living room that we didn't even notice it anymore. My mother had finally met her match, and even though she would inevitably win, I had a fabulous time egging her on. Soon the time would come to take the tree down, and I knew this when my sister told me that my mother's prayer chain was praying for it.

When March rolled around, I decided that I would take down the Christmas tree as soon as I had time, because it wasn't going to be a quick thing. It had grown stiff and sharp, and touching it was somewhat dangerous and was liable to hurt in the form of scratches and small lacerations. Although it was still green in spots, it drooped in a bunch of places, and if a little breeze blew by it, its needles would fall off.

So the ornaments came off, and we packed them away carefully. We unstrung the lights and put the tree angel back in its box. Soon the tree looked as naked as it did the day I brought it home in the trunk of my car, except that all the life had dribbled out of it. When all the decorations were gone, my husband asked me where the saw was.

"We can't cut up the tree," I said sadly. "It's been the focal point of my mother's life to mutilate it like that. She doesn't give her grandchildren this much attention. Let's take it to the recycling place."

He agreed, so we dragged it outside, popped open the trunk

of the car, and stuffed it in. We hadn't even backed all the way out of the driveway when the tree sprang out and rolled into the street. My husband got out of the car and mashed it back into the trunk.

"How far is this place?" he asked, now scratched and covered in Christmas-tree sap.

"It's right around the corner," I assured him, watching the scratches on his arm become red, raised, and swollen.

We started the car again, got out of the driveway and onto the street. We made the turn around the corner. Then we heard

THUD again.

The tree had escaped and was now positioned in the very middle of the street, blocking both lanes of traffic.

We pulled over to the side of the road and looked back. The river of cars migrating from the church down the street was heading toward the tree, *closer, closer, closer,* then swerving to the right to miss it, swerving to the left into oncoming traffic. Car after car suddenly jolted in either direction to avoid the tree, and one man in a truck just plain ran over it. We were trapped by the traffic for a long time, and neither one of us could do anything. Suddenly, my husband flew out of the car and retrieved the tree, dragging it across the street, and, for the third time, shoved it into the trunk. We drove, very, *very slowly,* mind you, an additional thirty feet, and dumped the Christmas tree next to its fellow dead Noble and Douglas Fir cousins at the Christmas Tree Graveyard, where tinsel gathered in muddy puddles next to the corpses.

The following day, when the doorbell rang, I sprinted to the door and flung it wide open.

"LOOK!" I shouted. "Look, Mom. It's gone. It's gone! Now I can finally do some welding in the living room! We're going to set off some firecrackers later!"

"Oh, yeah," my mother said, nodding. "God, it must have been more brittle than I thought. Look at all of the needles it left behind. It's like a carpet of little green pins! I hope the cat doesn't walk on them. What if one gets in his paw? That will be a hell of a vet's bill, I'll tell you. That could cripple him. When are you going to clean it up?"

"I'll clean it up soon," I sighed.

"You'd better," she whispered.

Christmas Death Trap

The truth was that I felt sorry for the two little girls from down the street, Casey and Staci.

I don't know, maybe I'm a sucker; maybe I'm just too gullible. Nevertheless, I must still hold tight to the theory that a six-year-old child at my front door asking me to feed her because her mother hasn't gotten out of bed in two days qualifies for a Sally Struthers kind of tragedy.

I had met the girls a couple of months earlier when they, one of them fully dressed as a ballerina, wanted me to pay them to cut my bushes, though I politely declined. My regular gardener was a forty-year-old man who equates a properly trimmed bush to a stump, and I knew I wouldn't have much more luck with an eight-year-old and a six-year-old.

After the bush incident, the kids started coming around in

the afternoon, and within a week of our meeting, it had become a daily ritual. The chimes would be tinkling, yet no one was visible through the front-door window. That's when I knew the midgets, as I started to call them, were getting hungry.

But soon, feeding them simply wasn't enough. They started bringing their dog to my house for Snausages and dinners of Kibbles and Chunks. Every time they set foot through the front door, one of them would spot something she liked, pick it up, and ask, "Can I have this when you die?"

This begging thing was obviously either a genetic trait or a habit picked up from their mother's fourth husband. One day, while disposing of all the unnecessary items in our house, I came upon the dusty, 1973ish fake-wood headboard that had belonged to my sister's old boss. Somehow, after the boss's father had died in the bed, we had assumed possession of it. I was quite ready to get rid of it, so I dragged it out to the front yard, slapped a huge FREE sign on it, and waited for someone to pick it up.

Within a half hour, the headboard was spied by the fourth husband, whom I call "Jethro," while en route to dropping both Casey and Staci off at their natural fathers' homes for the weekend. He sent the midgets up to the door to tell me to take the sign off the headboard while he smoked a cigarette at the end of my driveway.

After that, I came up with a whole bunch of ideas to trick Jethro. I toyed with the idea of dragging all of my trash, lawn clippings, and broken appliances to the curb and taping FREE signs to them so I wouldn't have to take them all the way to the Dumpster in the alley. Jethro, however, had beat me to the punch by hauling a plaid burlap love seat with missing cushions out to the dirt plot that was his front yard, appropriately accompanied by a broken dryer. As a matter of fact, Staci had been missing for several hours one afternoon until I saw her older brother open the door to the dryer and yank her out.

I bet, I thought to myself while driving past their house, that if I moved the dryer and the love seat to my yard and put FREE signs on them, the fourth husband would take them back inside the house.

I just hoped that they'd move soon, but they couldn't have moved soon enough. One Sunday morning, the doorbell rang, but as I peered from the hallway to the front door, no one was visible. It was the midgets, probably wanting breakfast.

Despite the fact that I was still in my pajamas, I opened the door, hoping to get rid of Casey and Staci quickly, but as I did so, I knew I had been trapped.

There they were, dressed in the same clothes as the day before, but this time, on top of Staci's right shoulder was perched a big, fat, filthy, dirty pigeon.

I shuddered immediately. I avoid birds, I avoid them at all costs. I've never had a simple, noneventful encounter with a bird and never will because of karma. I killed a bird with my car several years ago, and since then, birds have been shitting on my head, getting trapped in my air-conditioning vents, and being generally bothersome. To me, seeing a bird is like seeing the Antichrist appear before my eyes.

"You're not bringing that thing into my house," I told them right away.

"This is Petey. He broke his wing, and we're taking care of him. See?" Staci said, stretching out the bird's wing so I could see just how broken it was.

"Then he needs to be at your house resting," I said back.

"Isn't he pretty?" Casey said, stroking the bird's head.

"Nothing is pretty if it carries more vermin and disease than rats," I informed them. "And that's what pigeons are: big, fat, flying rats that shit—I mean, *poop*—on people's heads. Now take it home, girls, and make sure you wash your hands with gasoline."

Reluctantly and saddened, the midgets turned around and headed back down the driveway with Petey. I headed into the kitchen, ecstatic that I had successfully slipped away from a bird unscathed.

Within moments, I heard screaming from outside. As I listened closer, it was the terrified shrills of the midgets, calling my name over and over. As much as I wanted to ignore their cries for help—as much as I wanted to plead the case of "I'm Not Your Mother, So Go Drag Her Drunk Ass Out of Bed"—

I opened the side door and voluntarily, although quite hesi-
tantly, surrendered myself to the Midgets' Lair of the Filthy Pigeon.

I didn't want to go outside.

There was danger outside.

Simply concerned that the pigeon had turned mad and had
plucked out one of the girls' eyeballs, I rushed outside to
the front yard, where both girls were burrowed under the
bougainvillea bush.

"Help us, Laurie, help us!" Casey screamed. "Petey got
away, and he's under the bush! We need to cut it down!"

"Uh, no, we don't," I replied, crouching down until I could
see the bird underneath the bush, moving around and spread-
ing his vermin about. "First of all, stop screaming. Now, one of
you get on the other side and we'll flush him out."

Staci ran around to the other side, tunneled under her end of
the bush, and immediately shrieked, "PETEY! PETEY! PETEY!"
which naturally caused the bird to quickly scuttle over toward
my direction. Against my better judgment, I caught it.

"Here," I said, thrusting Petey at Casey. "Here's your bird.
Now go straight home and keep him there."

The girls gathered him up and started home. They weren't
one step out of my driveway when they began screaming again,
and I turned around just in time to see Petey, in a desperate
waddle, escape out into the street.

Both girls began to cry hysterically, and their yelling became even more high-pitched when they spotted a car eight blocks away.

"AHHHH! He's gonna die! He's gonna die!" Staci kept yelling. "LAURIE! You have to help us! Oh, NO! He's gonna die!"

Suddenly, there I was in the middle of my street, wearing a T-shirt and no bra and striped pajama bottoms, barefoot, hunched over, chasing and trying to capture a filthy bird that I hated. The more the girls screamed, the faster the bird waddled until I was almost breaking into a jog behind it, my arms outstretched and my boobs flopping around, completely unharnessed. My mother, unfortunately, was right. Eight hours of extra support would indeed go a long way.

For two blocks, I ran after the bird down the middle of the street as he wantonly ran for freedom or the next best alternative, the car. I couldn't blame him. I, too, would have gladly thrown myself in front of a speeding vehicle if my destiny rested in a shoebox located anywhere in that family's house. Casey and Staci ran slightly behind me, hollering and howling, tears shooting down their faces.

Finally, I cut the bird off, forced it in the opposite direction, and corralled it back into the yard belonging to my most dangerous neighbor, Frank.

Frank, in a pathetic attempt to deny that Christmas was indeed over, although it was now February, still retained his handcrafted holiday finery in his yard. This included a barrage of plywood Santas, Snoopys, snowmen, and elves with yellow eyes. Frank informed me that he had electrically wired his yard with enough volts to "knock a horse on its ass" in an effort to thwart potential thieves from stealing his decorations. I knew the capture had to be cautious to prevent electrocution, and I spotted Petey hiding between two gargantuan reindeer.

I made the only safe decision I could.

"There he is, girls!" I yelled, pointing. "Go get him!"

They both dove in between Donner and Blitzen and wrestled Petey as his broken wing sadly flapped in a fluttering panic.

"We got him!" they both yelled as they jumped up.

"Good job!" I nodded. "Now take him home, quickly. *Run!* And if you ever bring another animal to my house again, I'm calling the foster-care people."

I didn't see the girls again for a week. Then the doorbell rang; it had to be the midgets.

When I opened the door, they both looked sad, their faces long and their eyes drooping.

"What's the matter?" I asked them. "Is Petey okay?"

"My dad said he got better and flew away," Casey said.

And I bet you guys had "chicken" for dinner sometime this week, I thought.

"We're moving today," Staci said. "We're leaving at lunch-time for our new apartment."

"We wanted to say good-bye and give you a hug," Casey said. "We're going to miss you."

If I had been premenstrual, I probably would have cried. I did feel bad, though, and I wondered what the hell was going to happen to these kids, but I already knew. Each of them was probably going to have four or more kids by different fathers by the time they were twenty, just because they didn't know that their lives could have been any different. There was nothing I could do about it, anyway.

"My mom has a magazine with your picture in it," Staci said. "And we're going to keep it so we can look at you."

"Really?" I laughed.

"Yeah, and I decided something," Casey said. "I think I want to be a writer someday. Just like you."

What the hell is this? I thought. Am I trapped in some *Hallmark Hall of Fame* movie? Who wrote the script for this? Danielle Steel? If God wanted to put a lump in my throat, why didn't he just hit me in the neck with a softball or a brick instead of making little kids do his dirty work?

I had no choice but to let them in the house, where I proceeded to give them everything they asked for, even though I wasn't dead yet. I had to get a grocery bag because they wanted so much stuff, including a dusty old seashell, smelly soaps, a can of tomato soup, and a stick of margarine.

"Thank you," Casey said. "But we have to go now."

"We have to get ready for the new apartment," Staci added.

"Well, remember one thing," I told them. "When you guys get to be twelve, and your mom asks you what you want for your birthday, you tell her you want—now, can you remember what I'm going to tell you?"

They both nodded.

"You tell her you want Norplant. Okay?"

"What's Norplant?" they asked.

"It's insurance," I answered.

With their bags of my household possessions slung over their shoulders, they left for home. In three months, I knew, they wouldn't even remember who I was.

I wish I was that lucky. To remember them, all I have to do is look down the street into their front yard to see the burlap love seat and the dryer their fourth dad left behind.

The Most Unfun
Christmas Party Hostess Ever

There was no doubt about it. I had a choice to make, and it wasn't going to be easy.

I had had no idea the evening was going to end this way, with me locked in a vicious battle I was almost sure I'd lose. After all, it was just a Christmas party, a little, quiet get-together my husband and I had thrown for friends. Seven hours earlier, I'd had no idea that I would need magic, bait, and extreme forms of trickery on my side just to be able to go to bed.

Seven hours earlier, everything had seemed so innocent while we were waiting for our guests to arrive. I put the last of the dips out on the table as my husband did some last-minute tidying up in the living room.

"Hey!" he called out excitedly. "Do you think if I put my new

Emily Dickinson biography on the coffee table that it will spur some conversation?"

"Absolutely," I replied, moving the potato chips closer to the tortilla chips. "I have no doubt that later in the car ride home, most of our guests will debate whether or not I know that I married a gay man."

"I'm leaving the Walt Whitman *in my office*," he huffed. "And I'll even be amazed if anyone comes, since you are The Most Unfun Christmas Party Guest in this town, and everyone knows it. What time should I tell everybody that we're shutting down the party because the authorities are intervening this year?"

"You shut up! That is not fair," I cried. "That is an unjust accusation, and you know it! None of that was my fault!"

"Sure, none of it was your fault," my husband agreed, nodding. "Except the part when you picked up the phone and pushed 911 and the police came. You turned us all in!"

Unfortunately, my husband's memory of the ill-fated Christmas party was missing some rather vital details. Before we started dating, we had worked together at a record distributor, as did a majority of our musician friends who could not secure gainful employment elsewhere. In the middle of our work holiday party (which was held at the home of the company's owner), while everyone was having a great time, I was summoned to the bathroom by a co-worker because of a mysterious "emergency."

When I opened the bathroom door, there was another

co-worker and drummer, Steve, sitting on the sink, sweating profusely and mumbling incoherently. I didn't know why I was summoned instead of anyone else, and I figured that it was because I was one of the few girls at the party and because I was the receptionist, plus all boys know that girls are smarter, as well as prone to respond in a slightly more proactive manner when it comes to emergencies.

On second thought, I suppose it wasn't really the middle of the party, because unfortunately, the party really only had about three and a half more minutes of life left to live.

Now, in the bathroom, Steve's eyes were rolling around in his head, and at one really alarming (and admittedly unflattering) point, they went all zombie white. I asked him what was wrong, but instead of answering, he lurched toward me and then fell onto the floor. As he reached in my direction, I noticed that he was shaking, and I started to worry. His lips were moving, as if he was trying to say something, but no sound came out. Oh, God, I thought. Seizure. *Seizure!* He's having a seizure and the only thing I know to do for a seizure is hold the person's tongue so he doesn't bite it off and then bleed to death or choke on his own spit or something like that. And I so didn't want to do that. I mean, he was a nice guy, I liked him and we usually had fun drinking at the bar, but how much do we really know about our co-workers' oral hygiene? Oh, dear, I thought, it really is unfortunate that you're not in the wreckage of a fiery car crash—I'd have no problem pulling you from that, because

I wouldn't have to worry about what had gone into that mouth, or how slimy it might be, it could be like touching a huge, warm slug. And if my hand came back with some gunky stuff on it, that would be the gross-out of a lifetime, and in some ways, you could never come back from that. I'm just being honest here. You could never fully return to the person you were before part of your body returned marked with residue from Plaque Cove. I would never even want to grab my own tongue, let alone Seizure Steve's, but I knew if I let Steve die in front of my boss's toilet, that would, in many ways, be worse. So I got ready to make the plunge, put my right hand in a pinching position in case his tongue was thrashing about like an eel in a shallow tub, and then I had the most magnificent brainstorm.

"Did you take any pills?" I demanded. "If you took anything, you'd better tell me now!"

Now, this may have seemed like a very assumptive and odd question to ask someone at a holiday work party, but at my place of employment, it was not. In our workplace, in fact, not only were drug tests nonexistent, they were laughed at, particularly by our boss, who had a black belt in Xanax and Valium. In fact, right before I had been summoned to the bathroom, I was hanging out on the patio with my friend Dave just as he had spontaneously thrown up and then became violently angry because he had just popped two Darvocets and was certain they hadn't had time to make it into his bloodstream. We were all impressed when he discovered he was right; after some careful hands-on detective work, he found the pills, and unlike Jonah, after a trip to the sink, they were returned right back down the hatch.

In the bathroom, however, it was clear that Steve was not as acute a drug user as Dave as he nodded his head sloppily to my question.

"How many?" I asked as I shook him heartily. "How many did you take?"

And to that, the drummer fluttered his eyelids and then apparently lost consciousness.

"Oh, thank God," I said, breathing a tremendous sigh of relief as I let him drop back to the floor. "You only OD'd!"

The sounds of "Steve OD'd, man," "Dude, Steve just OD'd," and "Steve just OD'd in the boss's shitter!" went rumbling behind me, and I turned to find six or seven guys—*including my future husband*—standing in the doorway of the bathroom, doing absolutely nothing. Well, that wasn't true—most of them, *and I won't say who*, were busy rifling through their own pockets taking inventory in case Steve was as good a pickpocket as he was a drummer.

Suddenly, my boss appeared as the guys cleared out, and he nodded toward Steve.

"What do you think?" he asked me dryly.

You know, I wanted to say, if I had any marketable skills at all, let alone the assessment skills of a paramedic, I wouldn't be answering your phone, making your copies, and cleaning out a year's worth of fish shit from your dumb 180-gallon aquarium, and by the way, I will gag and pretend to get dizzy and nearly pass out the next time you make me do it when I'm wearing velvet, too. And I wouldn't be lugging fifteen pounds of your mail to the mailbox down the road when it's 115 degrees out as you drive by in your air-conditioned Mercedes coupe. And I wouldn't have almost put my hand in OD Steve's mouth. I'd have a job where I would have to wear a bra and I'd actually have health insurance. Which would come in real handy for at least one of your employees right now.

I shrugged. "I don't know," I replied. "He said he took pills."

"Pfffttt." My boss nearly laughed. "If everyone around here who popped a little pill passed out, it would look like Jonestown."

I shrugged. "Better safe than sorry" was what I said.

That was what I said.

That *was all*.

I didn't even dial the phone. Never even touched it. But within seconds, the paramedics were there, Steve was being wheeled out on a stretcher, and the party was over. As soon as my co-workers heard that people were on their way who could spot dilated pupils from a mile away, they loaded up on what free food and beer was left and fled as if there was a rumor that there were parents coming home.

And it was all my fault.

Steve, of course, lived, although it had less to do with the workings of a stomach pump and more to do with the fact that he had never taken a single barbiturate; I later determined through the grapevine that he'd been brave with drink and was trying, albeit dismally, to make a pass at me. Apparently, when I didn't react to his green hue, pinball eyes, and clammy body with lust and enchantment, he was already on the floor and the act had gone way too far. With his plan now gone wretchedly awry, I guess he felt he had no choice but to see it through, fluttering his eyelids, pretending to simply go to sleep, and leaving the party in an ambulance. And even though he faked a nap, which I misinterpreted as an overdose, it was all my fault. It was not Steve but I who was branded The Most Unfun Christmas Party Guest, and then someone with limited artistic ability (suspect: Steve) drew a likeness of me on the bathroom wall at work as a superhero named Captain 911 who could ruin parties with a moment's notice.

"You look tired," Captain 911 was depicted saying to a guy with droopy eyes tapping a keg. "So I called the police! We should get you to Emergency!"

"Party's over!" Captain 911 exclaimed in a bubble in another frame as she held a defibrillator, ready to strike surprised-looking revelers sucking on a beer bong. "I think he just swallowed a Tylenol!"

From there, it was a brand that stuck, even years later in my own home with my own husband throwing my own Christmas party.

"You need to get your facts straight, mister!" I said, shaking a finger at my former co-worker who would have been content to let Steve die, even if there were many people at that party who were far closer to death's threshold than Steve was. "I was just trying to save someone's life by offering an opinion! What did you expect me to do?"

"He just wanted you to stick something down his throat," my husband shot back. "Although I don't think he ever would have guessed it wasn't going to be your wiggling tongue but your finger."

"I did not ruin that Christmas party," I insisted. "And if you say it again during the course of this party, I am taking the reserve Costco truffles out of hiding!"

It was not an empty threat—every year for our Christmas party, I buy a carton of chocolate truffles from Costco that are incredible, as velvety and delicious as they are hard to find. This year, I hit three different Costcos before I scored a box, and I'd be damned if I wasn't going to save a secret stash of them for myself. They're always the hit of the party, and I knew that if I wasn't proactive, hiding just a couple, I'd miss out on chocolate-truffle season completely.

And I wasn't wrong.

As soon as the first few guests began arriving and migrating over to the food table, mouths opened wide and fingers started poppin' truffles. This was particularly true of one of my husband's friends, Reinhold, who showed up swathed in a huge wool scarf despite the fact that it was 70 degrees and he was someone I honestly didn't really want to come to the party. He had always rubbed me a bit the wrong way, the kind of guy who had minimal talents but acted as if he were blessed by the gods on Mount Olympus. In fact, the talents he did possess, but was oblivious to, bloomed like they were on an IV drip of Miracle-Gro. These included his uncanny ability to call just as we were about to sit down to a special dinner and then proceed to ramble for an hour about a poem he just wrote or the new pattern of facial hair he was about to try, his tendency to talk for an unlimited amount of time without a response, and his ability, despite his full-grown man size, to become completely drunk on one beer like a high school freshman girl before puberty came knockin'. My Nana could hold her liquor better than Reinhold, but when Reinhold was drunk, Reinhold was always right, which, although nearly impossible, made him even more difficult to tolerate than in a sober situation due to the fact that when fueled, he had the endurance level of the Six Million Dollar Man.

Now, despising Reinhold the way I did was a tricky proposition, because my husband, being the nice guy that he is despite the fact that once at a workplace Christmas party my spouse would rather have kept sucking on free beers than save the life of a sweaty co-worker, liked him. And not only did my husband like him, but Reinhold had never been anything but nice to me, so it made any argument I had about not inviting him over null and void.

So I said nothing. I said nothing as Reinhold, after three sips of beer, surrendered a majority of his hand-eye coordination and dove into the chocolate truffles with a squeal usually reserved for girls who have just been named prom queen. Like an infant trying to feed himself, he dropped two truffles right out of his saggy hand onto my brand-new linen tablecloth, and as they rolled off the edge one after the other, they left a trail that did not escape remarks about their similarities to the private kind of skid marks. He ate so many truffles that the spaces in between his teeth began to fill with what looked like rot and gave him instant tweaker teeth. He gobbled up those truffles before most of our friends even showed up, and before I knew it, the only evidence that the truffles had even been there at all were the pooplike trails and the chocolate that was now vigorously eating away the enamel on Reinhold's teeth.

Thank God he slipped into the backyard, where my husband's friends had gathered and had set some logs ablaze in the fire pit. There, they chatted about the latest *Frontline* they had seen, what was in *Harper's* that month, their favorite Kenzaburo Oe novel, and I believe someone even made a nearly funny joke about foreign policy. The fire crackled, spit, and warmed everyone. My husband and his friends looked into the orange glare and reflected.

In the living room, where my friends gathered, I did my monkey impression, my best friend's husband threw himself on the carpet and then performed the best Worm any of us had ever seen, and we talked loudly about how excited we were to watch the Anna Nicole Smith Christmas special that was going to be on in six minutes because we had seen on previews that her toothless cousin Shelly got naked in a hot tub and then threw a couple of punches at guests at Anna Nicole's party in a "Holiday Brawl." My dog, who could not be coaxed outside, farted. We all laughed and two of us snorted in glee like little pigs.

Sadly, Shelly did not get naked but merely exposed her panties and growled, "Okay, who's gonna get me laid?" After no takers came forth, she rolled her low self-esteem into her fists and fought two girls who tried to comfort her, knocking them both down like a bear with one swipe of her paw. All that with her panties showing. It was entertainment gold.

Right when Shelly was in the middle of her One Woman Hillbilly Smackdown, one of my husband's friends, Blythe, walked through the living room on her way to the bathroom.

"Oh," she said curiously at the sight of crazy cousin Shelly in panties throwing girls into walls as Anna Nicole wailed at her to "chill out." "What show is this?"

Now, although every single head in that room turned toward Blythe, no one said a word. It simply wasn't our responsibility. If she didn't know, it wasn't really up to us to tell her. You see, our Christmas party, as it had done every year previous, split like a cell and formed two separate parties almost immediately: my husband's group in the backyard was the Dull and Smart Party, where you would probably be forced to learn something or make a donation to a nonprofit before you left, and in the living room was the Fun and Stupid Party, where you would gossip, watch a drunk hillbilly go crack-ass crazy on TV, and mock the Smart Party without pity.

You see, it was too easy. Blythe had entered the territory of the Stupid Party, and it was indeed a rich and seductive land. Outside, the Smart partygoers shivered and huddled close to the fire, inhaling smoke and making them all smell like singed hair. Inside, our fire roared heartily in the fireplace, but it was clearly for a decorative element and we had a chimney, thus avoiding black lung. Outside, they sat on wooden chairs or the firewood, or they stood up. Inside, we had upholstered furniture. Outside, there was talk. Inside, there was Anna Nicole and laughter, *glorious laughter.* And we were far closer to the food. It would have been too easy crack open our world like an egg, claim Blythe and taint her as our own. The lure, once we exposed it, would have been irresistible, and despite her job as the director of a social-service agency, we would have had her cracking white trash and Section Eight jokes in no time, guaranteed. We could have taken her and marked her with our scent (onion dip), doubtful that the Smart group would have sent out a search party for her and risk leaving the intellectual bonfire unless she was fetching a microbrew for someone. Converting her would have consumed all of a moment, just a second to rewind to a toothless, drunk woman in nasty panties bellowing, "Who's gonna get me laid?" and then it would be time to initiate our new member to the dark side with a pig snort, a monkey impression, and the Worm. But that meant we would have had to divvy up the onion dip and remaining snacks one more way, lose a portion of our sofa space, and, well, the Stupid Party isn't *all that* Stupid. We allowed Blythe to return to her rightful people, and curiously no additional Smart people wandered into our territory for the remainder of the night.

That is, until several hours later after my friends had left and I was cleaning up. I didn't know about my husband's party, but *my* party had been a raging success. The onion-dip bowl was scraped clean, and for me, that translated into happy party people. Outside, the fire had burned down to a couple of embers. My husband had collected bottles for recycling, and we were turning off the lights to get ready for bed. I noticed that the living room light was still on, and as I turned the corner from the hallway to shut it off, a small little scream escaped from my lungs.

"What?" my husband cried from behind me, struggling to run with his pajama bottoms down at his knees.

There, in the living room, sitting in my favorite chair, looking straight at me, was Reinhold.

"Where are those little chocolate balls?" he asked.

"I'd imagine they've made it to your small intestine by now," I said, catching my breath.

"They were good," he stated. "There aren't any left?"

"Well," I replied, noticing that the fringed edges of his hearty woolen scarf were blackened and singed. "Seems there was one party guest who ate them like they were green M&M's and he was David Lee Roth."

"Oh," Reinhold moaned. "That's too bad."

"Man, I thought you went home," my husband said from the dark shadows of the hallway as he pulled his PJs up.

"No," our lone party guest said. "I wandered away from the fire to experiment with some shadow puppetry to lavish on my fire mates, but when I came back everyone was gone."

I looked at my husband, who looked back at me and said nothing.

"Well, it sure is late," I said with a smile. "You're the only one . . . left."

"Legend has it that you can clear a party out in seconds flat," Reinhold said boisterously. "I must have been perfecting my wolf shadow when you called 911! Heh heh."

My husband smiled weakly. He tied the drawstrings on his pajama bottoms and moved into the living room. I knew that was it. We were done for.

"Hmm," Reinhold said, leaning over to glance at something on the coffee table. "Emily Dickinson. 'I heard a fly buzz—

when I died—' Whatever. Shut in, malcontent, weird chick. Never smiled once in any picture ever taken of her, you know. Couldn't figure out what to capitalize and not capitalize to save her life. And her use of ellipses! Oh. *Aggravating and nutty.* Makes me just want to *shake her by the shoulders* and scream, 'Let's send you back to grammar school, shall we, because you obviously failed the class that the school specializes in!' Ha ha ha. Most of her writings didn't even rhyme, which to me is nothing short of a cry for help. Again, I want to shake her and say, 'Keep my attention, will you, sourpuss? Give me a rhyme for 'content'!"

"Welllllll," my husband started slowly.

"*Bent!*" Reinhold called.

"But Emily Dickinson," my husband tried to continue, "in her time was one of the most innovative—"

"*Ferment!*" our lone guest sang out.

"You know, to really appreciate Emily Dickinson, you have to understand the era—" my husband attempted.

"*Content!*" Reinhold shrieked again. "Oh, wait, or did I say that already? I don't think so. *Content!*"

I decided to go to bed. And I did. But before I made my retreat, I kissed my husband good night and handed him the phone with a smirk and the words "Remember you have to wake up early tomorrow. At eleven after nine!"

But despite the fact that I had freed myself from the Reign of Reinhold, I couldn't sleep. He had made me so mad that

I did nothing but toss and turn for what seemed like an eternity, and after time passed, I finally looked at the clock. When I saw that it was 3:30 A.M. and my poor hostage of a husband still hadn't come to bed, I knew I didn't have a choice.

I put on my robe and went out to the living room, which sounded oddly and suspiciously quiet. That is, until I turned the corner and heard something of a rumble, then saw my husband, his head tilted over the back of the chair and his mouth wide open—at first, I thought Reinhold had killed him with a lethal dose of uncut boredom or by sucking out my husband's soul to feed his own empty one—but then, a moment later, my husband engaged in nothing but a full-throated snore. He was completely and utterly asleep.

Across the coffee table, in my husband's favorite chair, was none other than Reinhold. Reading the Emily Dickinson biography.

And there it was. My unfortunate destiny. People always tell you to marry a nice guy, but when you marry a nice guy, do you know what happens to you? You automatically become the villain, you become Cruella DeVil, no matter if you really are or not, because the nice guy is too nice to do the dirty work. And my husband, clearly, before he fell asleep, was far too nice to tell Reinhold to hit the road and had preferred to drool and twitch in front of him.

"Guess what?" I announced to Reinhold. "I remembered

suddenly that I have more chocolate truffles. There wasn't enough room on the dish for all of them, so I saved some in the fridge. I completely forgot about them!"

"Really?" he exclaimed as he sat up and salivated like an excited puppy.

"Yes," I replied. "But there's a catch. I am dying to see your wolf-shadow puppet! You can't let all of that practice go to waste! And I'll trade you a truffle for a show!"

"It won't work in here," Reinhold said, trying desperately but in vain to get an image of his howling hand to appear on a wall. "We'll have to go out back to the fire pit."

"No," I said as I shook my head. "The fire is out! Hmmmm. Where can we go, where can we go . . . maybe . . . the streetlight against our fence in the front yard will make a marvelous screen for you!"

"Oooooh, splendid idea!" he agreed.

"Okay," I said excitedly. "You go out and test it, and I'll meet you once I get the truffles."

Reinhold shot through the front door and skipped down the steps.

I got the secret-stash truffles, said my good-byes to them, and let them know it was for a good cause. Then I placed them outside on the porch and quickly ran back inside, where I shut the door, dead-bolted it, and turned off the light.

A moment later Reinhold's chewing face appeared in the window of my front door.

"Hey!" he cried as he knocked so loudly it woke my husband up. "Hey! You locked the door!"

"You and your wolf can huff and puff," I replied. "But you can't come back in. Good night, Reinhold. Go home."

"HEY!" he shouted, still knocking. "You are The Most Unfun Christmas Party Person ever!"

I looked at Reinhold through the glass. "As usual," I laughed. "You are absolutely right. And don't you forget it."

And then we went to bed.

Happy Holidays
from the Asshole Family

Dear Friends and Family,

Happy Holidays!

Looks like it's time for another edition of the Notaro Dispatch and time to dish some dirt on what fun we have in our lives! I haven't seen most of you since that last little "gathering" at our house several months ago. It sure was a surprise, especially since I thought my husband was planning a birthday party for yours truly! But nope, just a regular old intervention. It was great to see you all, even those loved ones who sat on me when the attendants buckled those restraints. Boy, what a night, huh? It certainly surpassed my wildest dreams (even the ones when I'm barricaded in my house fighting off a SWAT team!). I was only expecting a cake! And suddenly, whoa! There's a stun gun! Ha ha! Who would have thought you could all keep a little secret so well? Hee hee! Not I, not I, said the fly! No, not I.

No, we did not have a baby this year. But we did move a thousand miles away, thanks in large part to some of you (you know who you are!!) who could not have been more encouraging, sometimes to the point of loading our stuff up in the van yourselves weeks in advance! Wonderful friends, wonderful friends. Which brings me to the point of writing this letter. It feels like we might as well have moved to Mars considering how hard it is to get ahold of some of you guys nowadays. Boy! You move across the state line, and all of a sudden you've become a Dr. Seuss character! Laurie Who! Laurie Who!

Ha ha ha!

Well, as I'm sure you're all dying to know, our move went as smoothly as we could have hoped. Except for the part when we were driving near Redding, California, and I found a lump in my breast. I know, I know, I held my breath, too, and it was indeed a long, tense, quiet drive to the motel that night, and naturally, there were quite a lot of tears. My husband, miraculously, remained so extraordinarily calm it was as if nothing was horribly wrong at all. He is a pillar. Later that night, on the side of a busy highway in a Motel 6 with sticky carpets, I was a moment away from giving my husband permission to remarry, and was getting undressed when I saw a massive and brilliantly colored growth on my chest. Frozen with horror and the thought that I never knew cancer came in a vibrant Caribbean blue, I flinched when my husband swatted at it and it shot across the room and bounced off a wall, and then he went right back to watching a Jack Nicholson movie without a word! I know. A pillar, I told you! Turns out it was just an M&M stuck to my chi-chi. Damn ("dang" for the PG version of the Notaro Dispatch for all of the kids out there!) those renegade car snacks and their ability to imitate tumors, especially when they go sort of soft and squishy with body heat. It's just like touching bumpy, diseased flesh. We got a good chuckle out of that!

As soon as we drove up to our new apartment, I knew it was going to be a spectacular and wondrous event in our lives. I didn't know just how exciting it was going to be until we walked up to the front door with our dog, and who came out of the building but one of our new neighbors with *his* dog! Our dog, Bella, whom many of you are already acquainted with, got so excited that she immediately gave out her "pretend growl," smiled at the neighbor dog showing all of her teeth, and then jumped on the other dog, trying to kiss the dog's neck. It was so good to see her want to play like that, and if she could talk (boy, we wish science would hurry up and master that one!), we know she would have just been yelling, "Let's play, you silly neighbor dog! I'm gonna kiss you! Big kiss! Why is your dad screaming and pulling you away? Let's play! Let's play! Boy, and I thought my mom was mean!" Yes, sadly, our new neighbor's overactive imagination mistook Bella's friendly advances as aggressive, violent, and lethal ones, but he was one to scream about violence! Pot, meet black! You should have heard the string of profanities he hurled at us and seen the dirty look he gave us! Wow, howdy, neighbor, I said, and for your information, we are not the Asshole Family!! Our last name is none of your business!

Nasty looks or not, I decided that I was going to start the Hello Project and become friends with the people in my building. I took it upon myself to say hello to everyone I met, and if they didn't cordially respond, I'd yell "Hello!" louder, just so they would realize I was serious. *And I was serious.* Most of the time it worked, as I believe that diligence and the ability to catch people off-guard—used in combination—can have terrific and pleasing results. Sure, sometimes I'd have to throw in a hearty wave and, on occasion, tap the person on the shoulder as a gentle yet firm reminder, but in general, I was able to easily and happily convert most of my neighbors to "Hello!"

There were, however, some "Hello!" holdouts, and some people that were Hello Project–defiant. Stubborn, unfriendly people! You know, a neighbor who says "Hello!," particularly in an apartment building where looking out for your fellow dweller is not only important but an essential part of apartment life, is one who is most unlikely to leave candles unattended, convert a bathroom into a meth lab, or go on a concert-volume Supertramp (*Dreamer, you know you are a dreamer/Well can you put your hands in your head, oh no!*) binge like the guy downstairs after he's snorted a complete shitload (PG version: crapload) of

An Idiot Girl's Christmas

crystal and you know probably recklessly walks away from open flames that REQUIRE CONSTANT SUPERVISION.

Those are important qualities in people you are sharing walls with, you know. *Important qualities.* Of course, keeping their impatient paws off of my panties the very minute my dryer is done in the laundry room is an important quality, too. That's important. There's nothing as startling as turning the corner with your laundry basket on your hip to find an eighty-year-old stranger with her craggly, wrinkled pretzel fingers looping through the legs of your stained underwear that no bleach on earth could conquer. HEY. You've never done your laundry in public before, how the hell are you supposed to know that old people will touch anything in order to get to a free dryer? I was so shocked I couldn't even say "Hello!"

The other people who were "Hello!"-resistant in the building, however, certainly didn't have such a reason; no one was fondling their underthings or poking at their cotton crotch when a simple greeting was expected from them. There were two neighbors in particular who outwardly refused to engage in the Hello Project by completely ignoring me: Anna, a sullen, huffy art student who had a dog named Camille Claudel, and a guy down the hall who only ventured out of the building to stand by the front door to smoke and cough. He looked like an unfortunate character straight out of a Dickens novel, straddling the physical and the nether worlds, as he surely had a foot in one as he did the other. Over his skeleton was pulled the thinnest layer of skin and muscle required to sustain life, which was almost visibly drifting away from him as the seconds passed. His eyes were consistently watery and rimmed in red, and his lips were so chapped that I just wanted to reach over and brush the flakes off myself. I've seen people on telethons that looked healthier. And not once did I ever see him wear clothes; instead, he regularly wandered down and out the door in a dirty T-shirt tucked into pajama bottoms or sweatpants and his little Rocky hat, a navy blue knitted cap that never left his head. I don't even know if he had hair. He generally always appeared to have a thin veneer of long-standing filth on him, which just added to the overall appearance of his Cup O' Noodles existence as he sucked down his generic cigarettes and then faded back upstairs like an apparition when smoke began seeping through his most-likely-single layer of skin. One day I saw a glimmer of hope in him as he propped his Skeletor body up against the wall of the building and gave me a nod as I walked out with Bella. I realized my chance, made a move, and jumped on it.

"Hello!" I said, stretching out my right hand. "My name is Laurie."

He extended his sickly, yellow limb that was either nicotine-stained or hepatitis-laden and mumbled back that his name was Lyle. It was like shaking the hand of a baby. Limp, effortless, and, you knew, full of bacteria and possibly a touch of turd. Then he stretched his leather lips a little, and I took it as a smile, although chances were more likely it was in response to a pain pang from within that had suddenly bubbled to the surface. Lyle. Well, I thought, that's easy to remember. You're tall and skinny and look like a decomposing Lyle Lovett. I could remember that. And I did. From then on, every time I saw Lyle in the hall or on the stairs, I bestowed upon him a greeting that was bold and warm and cheerful. "Hello, Lyle!" I'd proclaim, and most of the time he would acknowledge my hello by shifting his watery red eyes in my direction. Honestly, I wanted more from him, so I felt it was appropriate to move on to the more familiar and gregarious "Hiya Lyle!" and I combined this, not with an ordinary wave, but with an arching sweep of my whole arm to let him know just how happy I was to see him, even if it was just because it was good to know he was still alive and that the brownish fluid seeping through my walls was probably just a water leak after all.

But apparently, our moment had been lost. Lyle just simply stopped responding and went back to ignoring me, despite the fact that I continued to greet him, although a little less warmly. Fine, I thought, fine. Break up with the Hello Project. Do whatever you want, LYLE, even though you really never even once said it. You were really never a part of it, anyway, you just wanted the benefits of "Hello!" without the actual *work*. That's fine, Lyle, when your body fluids eventually do start seeping from my wall, guess who's NOT going to be saying, "HELLO? 911? I think my neighbor is decaying!"

Then, of course, there was Anna, who honestly just could not
be bothered to say "Hello!" Compared with her, Lyle had the
exuberance and zeal of the purple Wiggle strumming a banjo
and singing, "Cocky Want a Cracker!" Anna was a cold fish.
After my initial attempts at helloing her failed to elicit so much
as a flinch, I tried a different approach. I usually only saw her
when she was on the grounds of the apartment building,
throwing the ball to Camille Claudel.

"Your dog is so smart!" I called to her as Camille Claudel
chased the ball, flags of spittle streaming from her jowls.

Anna said nothing. Didn't even look at me.

"Camille Claudel is the prettiest dog in the building," I pan-
dered. "That's what I think."

No response.

"Rodin was an overrated Play-Doh amateur!" I said in a
last-ditch effort, but Anna remained a well that had run dry of
emotion and neighborly love.

As I stood there as Anna ignored me, I decided that was it. I
was done wooing Lyle and Anna—if they didn't want to partici-
pate and be nice, then that was okay with me. Absolutely A-OK,
I told myself. Can't be troubled to say "Hello," because it's a
biiiiiggggg trouble, believe me. Takes so much effort. All you
had to do was say it back. You didn't even have to initiate, just
respond. You know, what's the big deal? HEL-LO. Two syllables.
HEL. LO. An investment of two syllables to let your fellow

neighbors know they can count on you because we ALL LIVE TOGETHER, the same old lady is touching *all* of our underwear! I guess you're just too cool to say "Hello!"

Fine. Sure. I can play that. If that's the way you want to be, then don't you look at my girlfriend, she's the only one I got. How do you like *that*?

Maybe you also can't say "Good-bye, Stranger. It's been nice. Hope you find your paradise!"

How'd you like that beating up through your floors day and night because the guy downstairs is not very nice and so drug-crazed that all he can relate to is a constant, excessively loud *Breakfast in America* loop from 1979, which is probably the last time the asshole felt any twinge of solace or ambition as he watched the thin strings of hope drift farther and farther from his grasp at the same time? It's like having Mackenzie Phillips living downstairs! They *whistle* on that album, you know, *there is whistling!* That is the kind of person who doesn't say "Hello!" Anna and Lyle! The kind of person like Supertramp Guy!

Why can't you say "hello!"? Why? What is the big deal? It's the neighborly thing! Say "Hello!" Do you want me to burn my apartment down, do you? THEN SAY "HELLO!" GODDAMN IT. SAY F***IN' "HELLO," OKAY? SAY "HELLO" OR THE NEXT TIME I LIGHT A CANDLE I AM LEAVING IT UNATTENDED!! I WILL WALK AWAY FROM IT AND GO INTO A WHOLE OTHER ROOM!

Just then, a miracle sort of happened.

"I'm sorry, did you say something?" Anna said as she suddenly turned, pulled the iPod earphone out of her right ear and then her left.

I shook my head as Camille Claudel padded over and swung some frothy spit on my leg.

"I can't usually hear anything when I have these on, but were you . . . were you just singing a Supertramp song?" Anna asked, staring at me.

I shook my head again silently, merely and infinitely relieved that she had not turned around a quarter of a second earlier when I was also flipping her off.

Suddenly, the front door to the building swung open and who was it that walked out and immediately propped himself up against the wall and lit a cigarette?

"Hello, Anna," he said, complete with a cheery wave.

"Hello, Kyle," she replied.

Oh, I thought to myself. Oh.

I quickly walked to the front door, entirely ignored Lyle, and was halfway up the stairs when I heard Anna say to Kyle (Lyle), "I think I just found out who's been playing all of that Supertramp."

I did not see this as an obstacle to the Hello Project; quite the contrary. If they wanted to start a satellite chapter in the building, I welcomed it, especially if I no longer felt I had to alert authorities if Lyle (Kyle) hadn't been spotted clutching a wall in several days. He was now someone else's Hello responsibility.

Lyle (Kyle) eventually moved out, and the day that he packed up his stuff, I spotted a gray, identical figure shadowing him everywhere. I thought, Well, what do you know, Lyle (Kyle) will be dead before that truck is packed; his ghost has already arrived and is about to take over, but it turned out it was just his dad. Anna, well, I still hate her guts.

In the meantime, we're looking for a house, and when we find the right one, I can't wait to have a whole new set of neighbors to say "Hello!" to.

Ha ha ha!

Hope your year has been equally as magical,

The Asshole Family

Acknowledgments

Dear Santa:

I know I've been on your Santa Shit List for a while, ever since we met at that work-related Christmas party and I confronted you about the tin dollhouse you brought me in 1974 and then I called your friend a midget, but as I have explained numerous times, little people make me curious and a couple of badly mixed mojitos and some Mexican Xanax can make any girl a little combative. ANY GIRL—even, I bet, Shelly Janes, who lived across the street and DID get a wooden Victorian dollhouse that year, despite the fact that my letter was far more compelling and descriptive. SO WHAT if she spent the whole summer with two broken legs in a body cast to correct being pigeon-toed? How is that *my fault?* I wrote "wood" in my letter, too, remember, "W-O-O-D," not "TIN PIECE OF SHIT FROM KMART WITH THE FURNITURE AND DOLLHOUSE FAMILY LITHO-

GRAPHED ON THE WALLS." It was like a Twilight Zone doll-house! What little girl wants to play with dolls that are impossi-ble to touch? Anyway, I was hoping that we could have worked past that, but the last couple of years' worth of treats for me under the Christmas tree have demonstrated that you are not especially interested in "growing our relationship in a positive direction." I mean, really, I know you are pissed, but honestly, coal in my stocking says enough. Going the extra mile and sticking a whole bag of Kingsford in a full-body girdle was a lit-tle nasty and somewhat personal, particularly the Post-it Note that expressed how the lumpy coal butt looked so realistic. Very merry, Santa, very merry, but P.S., I'll bet your ass doesn't look any better under fluorescent lights. Plus there are people out there who are way worse than me, and you know it, like the googly-eyed crazy shoplifting Runaway Bride who invited five thousand people to her wedding and then split because the seating chart was too hard. MORE PEOPLE HATE THAT GIRL THAN HATE ME. Stick some coal in those eye sockets, why don't you? Those black holes are each the size of a Weber ket-tle grill!

But that's not why I'm writing, although I really do think that the Runaway Bride deserves a wedding gown full of coal if you're going to play that game. I'm writing because now that I know the way you work, I don't want you putting some people on the Santa Shit List just because they know me. They are very nice people and deserve nice things under the tree, not a coal effigy of themselves that maliciously and deliberately points out their body flaws.

Those people are:

Bruce Tracy; Jenny Bent; my old man; my family; Jamie; Jeff; Kelly Kulchak; Adam Korn; David Dunton; Shari Smiley; Kathy White; Sonya Rosenfeld; Kate Blum; Jennifer Jones; Donna Passanante; Heather Megyesi; Aimee Dexter; Katharine Enriques; Pamela Cannon; Beth Pearson; Maralee Youngs; Amelia Zalcman; Laura Goldin; Kimberly Obitz; Meg Halverson; Bill Hummel; Theresa Cano; Kathy Murillo; Kartz Ucci; Doug Kinne; Kate; Nikki; Sara; Sandra; Krysti; Gary; Sessalee Hensley; Jules Herbert; Craig Browning; Duane Neff; Amy Silverman; Deborah Sussman; Cindy Dach; Laura Greenberg; Beth Kawasaki; Eric Searleman; Michelle Savoy; Charlie Levy; Patrick and Adrienne Sedillo; Charlie Pabst; Colleen Steinberg; Erica Bernth; Jill Anderson; Maryn Silverberg; Becky, Marie, and Rhonda from Fairfax; Bill Homuth; Sharon Hise; Changing Hands; every bookstore who hosted an event and CRM on the last tour who was so very nice to me (especially in my new hometown of Eugene); and bookstores everywhere for still stocking my books.

AND ESPECIALLY Tom Nevins, because this book was his big, fat, fun idea, and, naturally, the Idiot Girls, particularly the ones on the Idiot Girls Board, who make me laugh, spew out my Pepsi, make me want cake, and who have made our Idiot Girl world so very much brighter and a delightful, hysterical, and a little bit dirty place to be. I adore those girls and I am proud to be among them. They are the most wonderful, funny, supportive, and caring ladies ever, Santa, and if you mess with them, or any of the people on my Nice List, I'm not just going to call your friend a midget next time. My lumpy coal ass will be doing some kickin'.

laurie n.
www.idiotgirls.com

ABOUT THE AUTHOR

LAURIE NOTARO loves Christmas, despite the fact that last year she was the unfortunate recipient of a jar of previously owned bath salts and an XXL sweater with a snowman on it. She does not subscribe to the saying "It's the thought that counts" when the thought is actually "If I clean it off and put a bow on it, she won't know I used this," but she does think it's funny to call out on the Holy Night "Ho ho ho and a bottle of rum!" because it makes her mother mad. This is her fifth book.

This book was set in Quadraat Sans, a typeface designed by Fred Smeijers. His first Quadraat typeface was serified, and he successfully adapted it to a sans version without sacrificing its lively and humane character. Quadraat Sans had display qualities, yet it is efficient, making it equally suitable for texts. Fred Smeijers (born 1961) was educated in typography and graphic design at the Arnhem Academy of Art and Design. He has been designing typefaces since the 1980s.